Chappell's Special Day Sermons

Chappell's Special Day Sermons

Clovis G. Chappell

PULPIT LIBRARY

BAKER BOOK HOUSE Grand Rapids, Michigan 49506

CONTENTS

❈

Chappell's Special Day Sermons

I

THE CYNIC'S NEW YEAR
(NEW YEAR'S DAY)

"There is no new thing under the sun"
ECCLESIASTES 1: 9

HERE IS A MAN FOR WHOM LIFE HAS OBVIOUSLY grown stale. He has suffered heavy and tragic losses. Among these, surely one of the most pathetic is the loss of his new year's day. Of course January 1 came to him every twelve months, even as it did to others. But it had for him no thrill of expectancy. It never meant a resurrection of hope. It never brought a revival of courageous effort to attain the heights. No longer did he allow himself to be betrayed by it into making rash resolutions for the achieving of the impossible. In fact this day had ceased altogether to be for him the beginning of a new year. It was only the beginning of another year of boredom and yawns, of disgust and despair, of wearily trudging through a monotonous waste of desert sand.

Now, the trouble with this man is that he has allowed himself to become a cynic. His cynicism is bold and pronounced. He calls himself the preacher. Be-

9

ing a preacher, he follows the time-honored custom of taking a text. Of course a good text is the first step toward producing a good sermon. But this preacher is not at all happy in his selection of a text. He does not select a passage that is warm with a sense of the love and fatherhood of God. He does not select one that is radiant with the expectation of the coming of a better day. No more is his text buoyant with the bracing assurance that the life that has lost its tang may recover its freshness and buoyancy. On the contrary, his text is about as sunny as a sob. It is about as hopeful as a wail of despair. Listen to the bitterness of it: "Vanity of vanities; all is vanity." No wonder that for him there is no new thing under the sun.

I

How has he come by his cynicism? I do not think that it is born merely of ignorance and inexperience. He is no youthful student just in from college, eager to impress his elders with his superiority. I do not take it that he is trying to shock us with his bold and daring wickedness. We are never greatly startled by hearing some young chap swaggeringly boast of his unbelief. We are not greatly frightened when he utters wisecracks as to the worthlessness of life in general. We realize that often he is only a little puffed up over his superficial knowledge; that he is perhaps wiser now, at least in his own estimation, than he will ever be again. Often, too, he is only parading in the borrowed garments of cynicism. But such is not the case with this man. His is far more than a mere pose.

No more is this man a cynic because he is passing through a temporary fit of the blues. The best and strongest men sometimes lose heart. Elijah was a man of tremendous courage, but he ran for his life one day, to fling himself down under a juniper tree and request for himself that he might die. John the Baptist was a man of colossal strength, but after days spent in a dungeon he began to wonder seriously if his whole ministry as the forerunner of the Messiah had been no more than a tragic mistake. But these men were not at their best. Often we utter sentiments in our hours of depression of which we are heartily ashamed when we come to our more normal days of sunshine and hope. But the cynicism of this preacher is far more than a passing fit of depression.

There are also those who become cynical through some great disappointment. Dean Swift was such a man. He dreamed a big dream of power, but the prize that he sought to grasp somehow escaped him. He did not take his defeat cheerfully. He became exceedingly bitter. Disappointed by the world of men, he sought to get back at them through the sharpest and most cutting of sarcasm. "His laughter jars upon us," says Thackeray, "after sevenscore years. . . . . He was always alone, alone and gnashing, except when Stella's sweet smile came and shone upon him. When that went, darkness and utter night closed over him." He was embittered by a great disappointment. But this was not the case with the preacher. So far as we know he had realized all his ambitions to the full.

Then there are those whose lives are darkened by great suffering. Job stood up bravely under blow after blow. At last pain laid hold of him and tortured him with unspeakable anguish. It was then that he lost his grip. It was then that he cursed the day that he was born. It was then that he looked eagerly toward death and to a resting place in the grave where the wicked cease to trouble and the weary are at rest. But his wail of despair was tortured out of him by the cruel fingers of desperate pain. Many a man on the rack has confessed to that of which he was not guilty. But this cynic, so far as we know, was in perfect health, and had never been the victim of any physical suffering.

Why, then, I repeat, is this man a cynic? He would have us believe that his is a deliberate and reasoned cynicism. And in a sense this is true. He is the type of cynic that has least excuse for existing, for life seems to have dealt kindly and bountifully with him. He has not been scourged into his cynicism by bitter suffering and heartache. He rather tells us that having tested the things that men think most worth-while, he has found them to be vanity; that having done much experimenting in the laboratory of life, he finds no other position than that of cynic possible. But in reality his cynicism is not so much a child of the head as of the heart. His real trouble is that he has no faith

12

in God. Being without God, he is natually also without hope.

II

What are some of the things that he has found to be vanity?

1. This physical universe. Other men have looked about them in this marvelous world and have been made to wonder and worship. The psalmist, as he looked into the heavens, heard them "declaring the glory of God." Addison, looking into the same heavens and watching the stars in their courses, sang:

> "What though in solemn silence all
> Move round that bright celestial ball;
>
> .   .   .   .
>
> In reason's ear they all rejoice,
> And utter forth a glorious voice,
> Forever singing as they shine
> 'The hand that made us is divine.'"

And Mrs. Browning found earth literally "crammed with Heaven and every common bush aflame with God." But when this preacher looked he saw nothing to give him a thrill. He saw nothing beautiful or exciting. He could not look at earth or sky without stifling a yawn.

"O world as God has made it! All is beauty!" sings Browning. "No such thing," answers this cynic. "I see no beauty in it at all. Why, look, the winds move in circles. The breeze that fans your face today will come back tomorrow. It never gets anywhere. The rivers flow into the sea, but the sea is never full because the water is carried back into the hills and poured out into the rivers again. Therefore the waters are moving in circles. The sun rises in the east and sets in the west with monotonous regularity. The petty race of men are toiling heatedly at the same tasks at which their dead fathers have toiled. The whole business is a wretched treadmill, about as purposeful and exciting as a squirrel chasing itself in a cage."

2. Pleasure. This cynic gave himself to the task of having a good time. His resources were abundant. He flung himself into the enterprise with abandon. There was no pleasure from which he held his hand. Every road that gave promise of a thrill he traveled. But he comes back from all his quests spitting the ashes of his burnt-out hopes from his lips and saying, "Vanity of vanities. There is no new thing under the sun." And it is a pity that every votary of pleasure in this amusement-mad day would not read and take to heart at least this much of his confession.

3. Achievement. This man set himself to the task of doing things that the world counts most worth doing. He became a builder. He constructed palaces. He beautified cities. He changed landscapes into gardens. The wilderness and the solitary place became glad at his touch, and the desert rejoiced and blossomed as a rose. In addition he amassed a vast fortune. He heaped up silver and gold. He possessed himself of a

great retinue of slaves. But when he had completed all the enterprises to which he turned his hand, again he muttered in disgust, "Vanity of vanities, all is vanity!"

4. Wisdom. Next the preacher set himself to acquire wisdom. One province of wisdom is to know. By experimenting in this field he reached the conclusion that wisdom is better than folly, as light is better than darkness. But he discovered that because the wise man knows more than the fool, he also suffers more. Therefore, he concluded that it is better to be a happy fool than a wretched wise man. Naturally he flung away from wisdom as a vain and futile thing, for, of course, "where ignorance is bliss, 'tis folly to be wise."

Then wisdom means not only the power to know, but to put knowledge into effect. It is power to be. To gain wisdom is to gain virtue. It is to win goodness. But he decided that this was also vain, since goodness met no reward. In proof of this it is striking that he appeals to the experience of another rather than to his own. Being good was not quite in his line. He tells, therefore, of a poor wise man who saved his city. "But," says he, "nobody appreciated him." And if he met no appreciation at the hands of men, neither did he meet any at the hands of God. Therefore, to be wise is absolutely useless. It brings no reward, either here or hereafter. "How dies the wise man?" he asks. "Even as the fool." And both of them die as the beast. The wise, the fool, and the beast all end in a common heap of mud.

5. Man. The preacher reached a desperate conclusion that man also is vanity. This is true for two reasons.

(1) Because mankind is almost universally bad. This cynic did not know any good folks. Being a man, and having some loyalty to his own sex, and deciding to spare himself, he said that there might be one good man in a thousand; but as for a good woman, such a thing did not exist. How lonely he must have been, being absolutely surrounded by vicious and wicked people, and being himself about the only decent man alive.

(2) Then, not only are men uniformly bad, but they are doomed to stay that way. "The crooked," he declares, "can never be made straight." To my mind this is by far the most cynical, the most utterly hopeless thing that he says. The Bible teaches the fact of human sin, but it teaches with equal emphasis that man may be saved from sin. The Bible teaches that men are lost, but it teaches with equal certainty that they are capable of being saved. But this man lived in a drab world of despair where the sinner has no possible chance of ever becoming a saint; where the prodigal can never leave the swine pen and find his penitent way back to his Father's house.

The truth of the matter is that the preacher's conception of man is not as a personality at all. He believes that man is a machine. The only God he knows is not a loving heavenly Father. He is a blind, grimy-handed fate. "There is a time for everything under the sun," he declares, and by this he means that man, the machine, has no power of volition, that he responds to certain stimuli without any freedom of choice whatsoever. This cynic you see is a Behaviorist. He is a profound believer in "the New Psychology. Therefore, naturally he concludes that "all is vanity and vexation of spirit." For we are

"But helpless Pieces of the Game He plays
Upon this chequer-board of Nights and Days;
Hither and thither moves, and checks and slays,
And one by one back into the Closet lays."

III

Now what was the practical effect of this lack of faith on the preacher's life? What did his cynicism do to him?

1. It killed all sense of obligation. He had scholarship and vast ability. But the idea that large capacity laid upon him heavy responsibilities to be of service to others was to his mind simply absurd. That poor wise man that saved his city only played the fool. In fact, to his thinking, all talk about duty and obligation was simply silly. He was vastly clever, but being without any sense of responsibility, he was, therefore, morally an infant. He was an intellectual giant, but he was also a spiritual dwarf. In secondary matters

he was keen; in matters of supreme importance he was little better than an idiot.

2. His lack of faith paralyzed all effort to help heal the world's open sore. What others suffered was none of his business, in the first place. His motto was, "Every fellow for himself and the devil take the hindmost." Then, how foolish to undertake to help folks when he is sure they are mere machines and cannot be helped. How stupid and futile to undertake to make the world better when he knows that what is wrong can never be made right and what is crooked can never be made straight.

3. His cynicism made him wretched. It took all the bloom and beauty out of life. It robbed him of all high expectation of the coming of a better tomorrow. It blotted out every star in his sky. It put him "on a rudderless raft in a shoreless sea." The one man to be congratulated, he thought, was the one that was dead. But better off, even than he, was the one who had never been born. In spite of all his efforts at pleasure, he had to say of laughter, it is vain. Finding nothing new, his biggest thrill is summed up in the one ghastly sentence, "I hated life." His best suggestion to you and me is to eat and drink. "Life is a tale told by an idiot, full of sound and fury, signifying nothing," he seems to say. "Therefore the best thing to do is to get drunk and forget about it."

There is a story of a man who was once pursued by a fierce beast. At last he took refuge in an old well.

When he was near the bottom of this well he discovered a horrible dragon with mouth gaped open, just waiting to receive him. Therefore he stopped his descent and clung to a little bush that grew out of the side of the well. With the beast above him and the dragon below him there was nothing to do but to wait developments. Meantime two mice came out of the side of the well and began to gnaw at the little bush. He saw that he would soon drop into the dragon's mouth, but during the thirty seconds that he still had to live he endeavored to sip a little bit of honeydew off the leaves of the bush to which he clung. This was somewhat the position of our preacher.

IV

But this cynic seems to have come to a discovery of God. Through this discovery his whole attitude toward life was changed. Through it all things became new.

1. Through the discovery of God he came to possess a new sense of duty. After this, he came to say "I ought" and "I owe." He closes his book with one of the most majestic sentences in the Bible. "Let us hear the conclusion of the whole matter: Fear God, and keep his commandments: for this is the whole duty of man." To discover God is ever to discover duty. The jailer did not notice the bleeding backs of Paul and Silas till he had found Christ. But having found

him, he took water the same hour of the night and washed their stripes.

2. Through it he came to a new sense of his personal responsibility. Discovering that man is a creature of obligations, he discovered also that he is to be judged according to the way in which he discharges those obligations. He no longer believed that the wise man and the fool meet a common fate. He believed the opposite. Therefore he warns emphatically: "Rejoice, O young man, in thy youth; and let thy heart cheer thee in the days of thy youth, and walk in the ways of thine heart, and in the sight of thine eyes: but know thou, that for all these things God will bring thee into judgment."

3. Finally, in the realization of all that he had suffered and of all that he had missed, he shows us how to avoid a like tragic folly. How magnificently he puts it! "Remember now thy Creator in the days of thy youth, while the evil days come not, nor the years draw nigh, when thou shalt say, I have no pleasure in them." Surely this onetime cynic is here speaking out of his own experience. He has lived through these pleasureless years against which he is now warning us. To him evil days have come, days that were dull and gray, drab and old. He has watched the sweet flower of life wither and rain its dusty petals upon the ground. "But it need not be so with you," he tells us. "Remember now thy Creator in the days of thy youth, and your sun will ever hang in a morning

sky, and life for you will keep its winsome newness from daylight until dark."

But if it so happens that we are no longer young, what then? Suppose we have already journeyed so far into the years that the call, "Remember now thy Creator in the days of thy youth," only mocks us with the glory of what might have been and now can be no more; then what has the transformed cynic to say to us? He does not insult our intelligence by telling us that our wasted years do not matter. He knows that not even God can do as much with the fraction of a life as he can with the whole of it. Yet he does not leave us hopeless. He gives us only so much of his command as we can bear. His call is this: "Remember now." However completely we may have squandered the year just passed, however listless we may be as we face the year just ahead, if we only dare to remember now, life for us will be remade. Instead of lamenting with the cynic that there is no new thing under the sun we shall shout with Saint Paul, "Old things are passed away; behold they are become new."

II

THE GREAT CERTAINTY

(EASTER SUNDAY)

"Beloved, now are we the sons of God, and it doth not yet appear what we shall be: but we know that, when he shall appear, we shall be like him; for we shall see him as he is."
I JOHN 3: 2

I

THIS IS A JOYOUS AND BRACING TEXT. IT HAS IN IT the deathless hopes and the high certainties that we associate with Easter. The author, the Apostle John, is looking out toward tomorrow. He is not thinking now of the immediate tomorrow, though to that he is never indifferent. He is rather looking toward that infinite tomorrow that he is sure lies beyond this world, with its light and laughter, with its griefs and graves. He is looking through eyes that are lighted by the radiance of Easter morning. What does he see? What is his attitude toward what lies beyond death? The answer is one that ought to bring a burst of spring to the most wintry soul. For his attitude may be shared by every one of us. It is the privilege of every genuine Christian. What is it?

It is not one of indifference. John does not dismiss all thought of what may lie beyond the grave with a careless shrug. "One world at a time!" is the popular cry of our day. We have become far more extreme in our hither-worldliness than were our fathers in their otherworldliness. Of course more or less indifference as to what lies beyond death is quite natural to the youthful. The reasons for this are obvious. They have been pointed out more than once. In the first place, to those who are in life's green spring, the life that now is seems entirely sufficient. It is a bit of an eternity in itself. So long as our sun hangs in a morning sky, we are likely to think little of what is to come at the end of the day. It is after considerable experience with life, often after the shadows grow long and we become conscious of the approaching night, that we begin to wonder just what may await us beyond the sunset.

Then in youth we have not passed through those experiences that make life after death so desirable to many who have reached maturer years. We have not yet come, through much living and working and suffering together, greatly to love. We have not yet stood by open graves that have taken into their grim arms those that we hold most dear. We have not been broken upon the wheel of life. We have not cherished hopes that long deferred have made the heart sick.

23

We have not yet bruised and broken the wings of our souls against forbidding bars that have shut us in and held us back from the realizing of our dearest dreams. It is natural, therefore, for those who are young to think little of what lies beyond the life that now is.

But such indifference on the part of those who have older grown is, I think, neither quite normal nor wholesome. It is genuinely tragic. This is true even when such indifference is born of a rugged self-discipline that has schooled its possessor to live without hope. It is even more so, when it is rooted in a profound selfishness. And this is often the case, I dare say, in spite of the fact that those parading such views tend to give an impression of unselfishness. The other day, for instance, a certain college professor was telling his class how utterly indifferent he was as to what lies beyond death. He put it even stronger than that, he expressed a preference for sleeping forever once his little day was over. Now, in my opinion, not a member of his class was greatly shocked by his statement. Nobody said, "How heartless! How utterly selfish!" For the most part, they rather seemed to approve, to say with admiration, "Here is one who is big enough not to be selfishly grasping at life as if he were essential to the ongoing of the universe."

But there is really nothing here to challenge our admiration. To be convinced of this it is only necessary to change the setting of the professor's statement. Suppose, for instance, that we pass from the classroom to the cemetery. Here arm in arm with him we stand beside an open grave. It is the grave of his mother. Now, suppose that, standing in this solemn presence, he should repeat approximately what he has just said in the classroom: "I do not care in the least whether there is such a thing as immortality or not. It is a matter of complete indifference to me whether my mother is as if she had never lived, whether she has now become 'a brother to the clod which the rude swain turns with his share and treads upon,' or whether she is consciously alive forevermore. In fact I really prefer that, now that her brief day is over, she shall sleep forever." Who would admire and applaud now? Who would not rather say, "How horribly heartless!" To John such indifference is utterly impossible. He has too big a heart. He is too much of a lover.

No more does John look toward death, and what may lie beyond, with terror. There are those, you know, who refuse to think of these matters because they dare not. The cold thought of the tomb is for them the skeleton of all feasts. This is the case because they never think of death as an exodus, a mere passing from one room in God's great house into a larger and a brighter. It is rather a blind alley that leads nowhere but into nothingness. It is a ghastly red light that either puts an end to all traffic forevermore, or guides the way to a yet deeper tragedy. It is said of Louis XIV that he never allowed death to be mentioned in his presence. That was the case because the very thought of it made him afraid. He shut his eyes to it because he dared not face it. But for John, it has no terror at all.

How, then, I repeat, does John face the future? He faces it with calm confidence. He faces it also with keen and eager interest. This he does, not because he claims to know all that lies beyond death. He does not claim to have a blueprint of heaven. The Bible is consistently and beautifully reticent about the afterlife. It does not undertake to tell us all that we should like to know. It makes no effort to satisfy our curiosity. This to me is an evidence of its truthfulness. I am not sure that such knowledge would be best for us. I am quite sure that it would be quite beyond our comprehension. John, therefore, is not afraid to tell us that he has no full knowledge of all that we are to expect when done with this present world.

For instance, he says, "We know not," or, "It has not yet been made manifest what we shall be." That is, I take it, John is confessing that he does not yet fully know the manner of life we shall live in that great tomorrow. He is sure of its reality, but of little else. But while he is ignorant as to the details he knows enough to make him at once both confident and eager. In fact his eagerness is heightened, not only by what he knows, but even more, possibly, by what he does not know. That is quite natural. Here, for instance, are two boys who are expecting Santa Claus. One is not only sure of his coming, he is also sure that he knows what he is going to bring. But the other is in entire ignorance as to what he is going to bring. His one big certainty is that he is coming. Which of the two will look to the event with the greater eagerness? Not the one who knows, but the one who does not know. Thus it is with John. Being sure of the afterlife, his ignorance as to details only makes his great expectation all the more thrilling.

II

But while John confesses his ignorance of certain details of the afterlife, he does not desire to leave the impression that he is entirely in the dark as to the whole matter. There are certain fundamental facts of which he is genuinely sure. "We know!" is his bold and bracing declaration. Of course his knowledge is not that of the mathematician. He does not know, as we know, that three times three make nine, or that a straight line is the shortest distance between two points. He knows, with a knowledge that is far more thrilling and far more satisfying than that. What are some of the things of which he is so sublimely certain?

1. Though he does not know what we shall be, he is certain that we shall be. He is sure of the survival of personality. He is firmly convinced that you will always be you, and I will always be I. He believes in the immortality of the individual. And that, by the way, is the only immortality that is reasonable. It was George Eliot who sang very beautifully about the immortality of influence, of living again in lives made

27

better by our service, etc. But such an immortality of influence requires, as others have pointed out, an immortal race. But where shall we find an immortal race? Surely not here. Science tells us emphatically that such is impossible becaus his world is passing on to a time when it will not be fit for habitation. Unless we live, therefore, as individuals, we cannot live at all. But John is sure that he is going to live individually, to be himself forever.

2. John is also certain that in the afterlife, his fellowship with Jesus Christ that has begun here, is not going to be broken, but is going to grow dearer and more intimate through eternity. "We know that we shall see him as he is," he declares joyfully. Here he has been privileged to walk with Jesus about the dusty roadways of Judea and Galilee. Here he has leaned upon his bosom. But even then, he has seen him but dimly. He has seen him with eyes that were dreadfully lacking in clearness of vision. There, all blindness will be taken away. There, he will see him as he is, and have fellowship with him forevermore.

When John wrote this, he was doubtless thinking of that solemn scene in the upper room years ago when he had sat with his fellow-disciples under the grim shadow of the cross. It had dawned upon them at last that their Master was going away. They were crushed. Their hearts were utterly broken. They saw nothing worth living for in the dull, gray days ahead. Then it was that Jesus turned to them with these healing words: "Let not your hearts be troubled; ye believe in God, believe also in me. In my Father's house are many mansions: if it were not so, I would have told you. I go to prepare a place for you. And if I go and prepare a place for you, I will come again, and receive you unto myself; that where I am, there ye may be also."

3. Then John is not only sure that he shall enter upon a richer experience of the fellowship of Jesus in the afterlife, but that this shall also be the privilege of all of his fellow-saints. Thus entering into a richer friendship with their risen Lord, he is further sure that they shall enter upon a richer friendship one with another. And this bracing assurance may also be ours. For, if beyond the life that now is we are to enter upon a greater intimacy with our Lord, we may be sure that we shall be privileged also to enter upon a greater intimacy with those that we love and lose. We shall know there, with a fuller knowledge than we have known here, and thus knowing, we shall love with a far deeper love.

4. Finally, John is sure that the afterlife is going to be one of eternal progress. He is convinced that the Christ who has exercised such transforming power upon his life in the here and now will go on exercising that power forever. What vast changes Jesus has already wrought within him. He is now known as the Apostle of Love. But he was anything but that when Jesus found him. He was a hot-hearted

man, full of lightning and thunder. He it was that swaggered into the presence of Jesus with this report: "We saw one casting out demons in thy name, and we forbade him because he followed not us." He it was that wanted to call down fire from heaven upon certain ignorant and misguided villagers who had refused himself and his Master a night's lodging. Certainly it is a far call from the John of that day to the radiant-faced saint whose one message has come to be, "My little children, love one another." John has made progress. Therefore, he believes, and has every reason to believe, that he will go on making progress forevermore. "We know that, when he shall appear, we shall be like him; for we shall see him as he is."

Thus it is evident that John does not believe in a static heaven. He does not believe in an afterlife that is little more than a long preaching service. The picturing of heaven as a kind of lotus land where we are to drowse in utter idleness has, I am sure, done much to lessen the interest of adventurous and eager souls. We yearn for the joy of going on. And that is what is offered in our text. How do we make progress here? By work. By conflict. By flinging ourselves into great tasks and great adventures. I am sure it will be so there. Only there, we shall work with more skilful hands, with hotter hearts, and with wilder joy. Therefore, we are sure that, working and achieving, we shall go on becoming increasingly like our Lord throughout eternity. What a blessed hope!

III

But what makes John so sure of all this? Upon what does he base his firm conviction? "We know that, when he shall appear, we shall be like him; for we shall see him as he is." "We know." How dogmatic! How daring! How little at home is such a claim today, even upon the lips of the saints! "We faintly trust the larger hope"; but as for knowing, that, we feel, is far too strong a word for the pale dream that is ours. But not so for this spiritual giant. "We know," he affirms with unshaken and unshakable conviction. "But how do you know?" we ask wistfully. For surely here is a knowledge that we should all like to share.

Now, when John undertakes to answer this question, he does not do so by any elaborate argument. But as we listen to him, this at least is evident: The foundation of his conviction is his certainty of the resurrection of Jesus. But why is he so sure of this? Here he makes no appeal to mere external evidences. He does not remind us of his visit to that empty tomb on a certain Easter Sunday long ago, when he saw and believed. He does not tell us that since the tomb was empty it must have been emptied in one of three ways —by the friends of Jesus, by his foes, or by a resurrection. That it was not emptied by his friends, because they believed he had risen, believed it strongly enough to preach it, and even die for preaching it. That it was not emptied by his foes, else they would have produced the body and ended the heresy. Since it was not emptied by either friends or foes, it must have been by a resurrection.

But John has nothing to say of outward evidences. This is the case, I dare say, not because he thinks that evidences are of no importance, but because he is sure that they are not enough. Once, as a boy, when too much company came, I was not allowed to eat at the first table. When I went to the second, I found abundant evidences of fried chicken, but, sad to say, I found little else. In fact, as I looked the situation over, there was no doubt in my mind that chicken had been served. The evidences were simply overwhelming. But in spite of this fact I was far from satisfied. And John is wise enough to know that the human heart can no more be satisfied by evidences of the risen Christ than the hungry can be satisfied by evidences of bread or the thirsty by evidences of water.

On what, then, does he base his certainty? He bases it upon a present experience. It is an experience that is intensely personal. It is one also that he is sharing with his fellow-saints. "Beloved, now are we the children of God." He is conscious in the here and now of sonship with God through Jesus Christ. Therefore he never thinks of Jesus as merely a beautiful memory. He never thinks of him as one whom he has loved and lost in the radiant long ago. He is a present reality. He is One whom he knows now and with whom he is now experiencing joyful fellowship.

32

"No fable old, nor mystic lore,
  Nor dream of bards and seers.
No dead fact stranded on the shore
  Of the oblivious years.

"But warm, sweet, tender, even yet
  A present help is he;
And faith has still its Olivet,
  And love its Galilee.

"The healing of the seamless dress
  Is by our beds of pain;
We touch him in life's throng and press,
  And we are whole again."

Such an experience does not do away with evidences any more than the sunrise destroys the stars. It only makes them seem secondary and insignificant. For John, therefore, argument about the reality of life in Christ seems utterly unnecessary. He no more needs verbal proof of it than a thirsty man would need proof of the reality of water when he was kissing a gushing spring upon the lips.

Now since John is in possession of eternal life in the here and now, he believes that this priceless treasure will be his forever. This does not mean that he regards eternal life merely as endless existence. He rather looks upon it, as do the other writers of the New Testament, not as endless existence, but as endless right existence. It is not a quantity of life; it is a quality of life. It is not to be ours simply when we die, but in the here and now. We possess it as we possess and are possessed by our Lord. He is himself the resurrection and the life. That is what he is to John now; that he is sure he will continue to be always. He cannot conceive of the Good Shepherd's going home in the gloaming and leaving his sheep to the terrors of night. That would mean either that he did not love us, or that death were stronger than he. John is sure of his love. He is equally sure of his power. And we, too, may be sure. Therefore we may join our voices with his this Easter morning as he shouts: "Beloved, now are we the sons of God, and it doth not yet appear what we shall be: but we know that, when he shall appear, we shall be like him; for we shall see him as he is.'

III

BELATED SAINTS [1]
(PENTECOST)

"All the baptism he knew was that of John"
ACTS 18: 25 (Moffatt)

ALL THE BAPTISM HE KNEW WAS THAT OF JOHN."
That is a rather surprising and startling statement
to read of one who has been instructed in the things of
the Lord. It becomes even more so when we realize
that the one so instructed has accepted that instruc-
tion and has actually become a disciple of Jesus. And,
while the spiritual requirements for the pulpit are no
greater than those for the pew, it becomes more surprising still when we realize that this man has not only
become a disciple, but has entered the Christian ministry. Yet, such is the case. Apollos is a preacher. He
is one of the great men of the early Church. He has
set himself to the tremendous task of remaking men
and of bringing in the Kingdom of God. But, sad to
say, he undertakes this amazing impossibility knowing

[1] This sermon was first published in part in *Great Themes of
the Christian Faith* by Harper and Brothers. It is reproduced here,
after being re-written, with their consent.

35

only the baptism of John. What inadequate equipment! How can he hope for anything better than heartbreaking failure? He has much, but he does not have enough.

I

Look at the wealth of his equipment.

1. He is a man of great native gifts. Now, we are not forgetting the fact that the bulk of the world's work must be done by us who are of mediocre ability. Nor are we forgetting that the man of one talent is just as worthy of honor as the man that has five. No man is to be crowned simply because he is gifted. Large gifts do not reflect credit upon the receiver, but upon the giver. But while this is true, it is also true that vast ability opens the door to vast usefulness. A consecrated million will surely do more than a consecrated penny. Therefore, we are glad to welcome into our brotherhood this man of outstanding ability. And we rejoice that through the centuries so many of the world's greatest intellects have consecrated their large gifts to the service of the Kingdom.

2. He is a man of fine culture. He is a native of Alexandria. This city, like the native city of St. Paul, was the seat of a university. It also possessed the greatest library of antiquity. It was a city of scholars and philosophers. Apollos has, therefore, been exposed to the finest educational opportunities of his day. Not only so, but he has made wise use of those

opportunities. Thus he has brought to the work of the ministry one of the best-trained minds of his day. So splendidly equipped is he both by nature and training that he is able to preach even in the pulpit of the marvelously endowed and cultured Paul. In fact Paul has to share honors with him. And no wonder. Such a preacher would be capable of winning a hearing in any age. In fact, Apollos, Paul, and Luke share the honor of being the three best-trained men of the early Church.

3. He is a man of flaming zeal. He has kept the hot fires of a fine enthusiasm burning upon the altar of his soul. That is splendid. The truly worth-while work of this world is ever done by the hot-hearted. It is these, too, who call out the best there is in us. The tepid, timid, half-hearted individual does little and makes little appeal to either God or man. And the burning ardor of Apollos is all the more dynamic because it is coupled with high culture. Unfortunately, outstanding scholarship and flaming zeal do not always walk arm in arm. There are those the chief ends of whose learning seem to be either to serve as a new kind of fire extinguisher or for cold storage purposes. Of course, this is not the fault of scholarship. Certainly we are not to conclude that the fine flower of zeal thrives only in the lean soil of ignorance. We have all known men like Apollos who were at once highly cultured and highly zealous. We have all known also those who were at once dreadfully lacking both in knowledge and also in zeal. Hot enthusiasm is good in any worthy

37

cause, but the more intelligent it is, the better. Therefore, we appreciate especially the zeal of Apollos.

4. He is mighty in the Scriptures. How refreshing! No disciple who aspires to a vigorous spiritual life can afford to neglect the Bible. Certainly no one who teaches in the church school or holds a position of leadership in the church can afford to slight this supreme book of mankind. But the Bible is the preacher's specialty. He is expected to be able to teach it with some degree of assurance and authority. Apollos has studied and read widely, but he has majored on the Word of God. Therefore, Luke could write of him that he was mighty in the Scriptures. We congratulate him and we congratulate those who were privileged to sit under his ministry. It is well for the preacher to be mighty in organization, mighty in financiering, but it is better still for him to be mighty in the Scriptures. It is such men whose ministry has ever been most rich in abiding usefulness. Bunyan has guided millions toward the Celestial City. This he has done, not simply because he was a genius at allegory, but more still because he was mighty in the Scriptures.

5. He is hospitable to the truth. He is eager and ready to learn from anyone who is able and willing to teach. That is his salvation. That is what kept him from squandering his fine resources for returns meager in quantity and poor in quality. Being eager to learn, he is, therefore, capable of teaching and preaching. To close the door of the mind is fatal. Years ago I knew

a young man of high possibilities who decided to enter
the ministry. His educational opportunities were of
the very best. His work both in college and seminary
was full of promise. But having finished his training and entered upon his chosen work, he seemed to
think that his days of toil were over. He quit reading.
He quit growing. He became a victim of arrested
development, a disappointment to himself and to others.

Apollos is different. He is possessed of an eager
mind and heart. He continues to learn and, therefore,
to grow. And what is more commendable still, he is
willing to learn about his own specialty, and that from
those who were doubtless far his inferiors both in ability and culture. Surely a rare man is Apollos. Were
I serving on the committee for securing a new pastor
for my church, I should give careful consideration to
this gifted, cultured, zealous, open-minded, and scriptural preacher. But having considered, I greatly fear
I should have to vote against him. This is true because Apollos has one great defect that, if left uncor-
rected, must cause his brilliant ministry to be little better
than a failure.

II

What is wrong with Apollos?

It is not that he is a heretic. No more is he a wild
and foolish fanatic. He has not been improperly instructed; he has been inadequately instructed. All the
baptism he knows is that of John. He does not know

39

the baptism of the Holy Spirit. He has not entered into that life-giving, transforming experience that came to his fellow-disciples at Pentecost. He is thus belated, completely behind the times spiritually. He simply has not arrived. He is not in reality a Christian at all. Therefore, in spite of all his lordly gifts, in spite of his commendable zeal, he is but poorly equipped for the great work to which he has set his hand. No man is adequate for the task of Christian living and of Kingdom building whose adequacy is not of the Holy Spirit.

This is the plain teaching of our Lord. "It is the Spirit that quickeneth." How well fitted were Peter and John after they had seen their risen Lord! They had companied with him during the days of his earthly ministry. They had seen him die. They had seen his tomb which was at the same time the grave of their dearest hopes. Peter had looked upon this grave with increased bitterness because of his cowardly denial of him. But a new day has dawned. It is Easter Sunday. Christ has risen—the same forgiving Savior as of old. He can hardly wait to get the door of the tomb open before he sends a special message to Peter and grants him a private interview. Thus the past is buried, and Peter has a wonderful story to tell. His fellow-disciples share his message and passion. But Jesus says, "Not yet. Wait for the promise of the Father. Tarry ye till ye be endued with power from on high."

And just as it is true that no man is adequate without this experience that Apollos lacked, it is equally true that to all who claim it there comes an amazing adequacy. We think wistfully at times of the privilege of those early friends of Jesus. How wonderful to have walked by his side, to have felt the touch of his hand, to have sat under the spell of his voice! No wonder that their hearts were crushed when they found that he was going to leave them. No wonder that they could not think of the empty, gray days ahead without their faces being wet by hot and bitter tears. But Jesus tells them, in his quiet way, that by going he is doing the best possible for them. "It is expedient for you that I go away. My going is the roadway to an infinite nearness." And, incredible as it seemed, they find it gloriously true. They realize after Pentecost that he is not only with them, but within them. He is now more blessedly near and real than ever before.

"All the baptism he knew was that of John." What a fatal defect, what a tragic loss! For this means that though he knows about Jesus, he does not know Jesus himself. He knows about him, but he does not realize him. He cannot say with Paul, "Have I not seen Jesus Christ, our Lord?" He cannot shout with him with unshaken and unshakable conviction, "I know whom I have believed, and am persuaded that he is able to keep that which I have committed unto him against that day." He has, therefore, missed the one supreme essential of Christianity. Knowing only the baptism of John, the Spirit is not yet able to take the things of Christ and to show them to him.

Being unable to realize Christ, he is alike unable to reproduce him. He has not become a new creation. He cannot say with the Spirit-baptized, "For me to live is Christ." He cannot sing, "I am crucified with Christ, nevertheless I live, and yet not I, but Christ liveth in me." Men do not take knowledge of him that he has been with Jesus. Wanting the Spirit, though he seeks to imitate Christ, he cannot incarnate him. Like so many today, he is simply undertaking to do in the energy of the flesh what can only be done in the power of the Spirit.

Of course, this sad defect tells upon his entire ministry. It tells upon his personal contacts and upon his preaching. He is an eloquent and forceful speaker. Those who hear him are instructed. They are doubtless thrilled and entertained. They are compelled to admire his many fine qualities. But in spite of all this, he somehow fails to bring them a sense of the presence of Christ. He does not compel them to say in their hushed and awed hearts, "Surely, God is in this place." Therefore, though a wonderfully attractive preacher, he is not a powerful preacher. Though eloquent and earnest, he is not greatly helpful.

It is evident that those choice saints, Aquila and Priscilla, are disappointed in him. They have doubtless looked with eager anticipation to his coming to Ephesus. Now that he has come, they go to the service with high expectancy. But the preacher has hardly begun before they feel that there is something lacking,

42

and they are very sure what that something is. They realize sadly that in his ministry to the saints this great preacher is little better than a failure. Nor does he seem to be more successful with those without the Church. We have no right to say, of course, that those twelve backward disciples that Paul found upon his visit to Ephesus were converts of Apollos. But this, at least, we may say: They are the kind of converts we should expect him to make. They are like him in their entire ignorance of the baptism of the Holy Spirit.

Now, many years have passed since then, years in which Christianity has spread around the world. But after all these centuries, we cannot shut our eyes to the fact that there are vast numbers in the Church today that are just as far behind the times as Apollos. In fact I am afraid that this distinguished minister would feel far more at home among a group of modern saints than among those of whom he was a part. It is my very firm conviction that the saddest lack of the Church today is that from which Apollos was suffering. We need his ability and culture, but there must be something more. If I were asked to point out the greatest weakness of the pew today, I should have to say "a lack of a vital religious experience." If I should be asked to indicate the greatest weakness of our increasingly efficient teaching force, I should have to give the same answer. If I should be asked the same question with regard to our ministry which is the best-trained the Church has ever had, I should have to give the same monotonous answer. Therefore, many of us are tired and harassed and discouraged. This is true because we insist upon undertaking in the energy of the flesh what we can only do in the power of the Spirit.

III

Is there a way out for Apollos? Is there a way out for ourselves? I am perfectly sure that we may answer in the affirmative.

Look at Apollos. He preaches the best he can, but is disappointing. But when the service is over Aquila and Priscilla do not pass the word along that the preacher is unsafe and that they had better refuse to give him any further hearing. Had they done so they might have worked a great injury both to the preacher and to the congregation. Instead they do that which indicates both consecration and tact of the highest order. They doubtless invite the preacher home with them for dinner. The meal over, they proceed to expound unto him the way of the Lord more perfectly. That is magnificent. It is hard to tell which to admire the more, the instructors or the instructed. It is certainly a delicate matter to instruct a preacher, for we are a sensitive tribe. Great credit is due these tactful teachers. But great credit is also due Apollos. He does not flash his diploma and his various degrees at them. Instead he listens with childlike humility. As he listens, his heart burns within him. He feels that here is good news indeed.

What, I wonder, do they say to this earnest man who is working so hard and doing so little? I think they tell him what has recently taken place at Pentecost. They tell him that Jesus who was so accessible to his friends in the days of his flesh is far more accessible now, that he has come again in the person of the Holy Spirit, and that he now offers himself to every man who will receive him. "This," they add, "is not mere theory. It is a fact of experience. We have tested it and found it true. We are finding it true even now. He is with us day by day and hour by hour as a living Reality."

And is not this just the message that you and I need? Being religious is such a chore for many of us. We often feel that in spite of all our wearying efforts we have made a bit of a mess of it. In our efforts to be like Christ we feel that we have been about as successful as if we had been out seeking that fabled pot of gold at the end of the rainbow. The nimble goddess of the mists has fled far faster than we could pursue. All that we seem to have won is torn garments, sore feet, and a yet sorer heart. What is wrong? How have we missed the way? Maybe our mistake has been that of Simon Magus. He thought that this Gift might be purchased. Of course we have not offered vulgar coin as he did. We have rather offered other values like earnest effort, a correct creed, strict orthodoxy. Or perchance, as Apollos, we have failed to hear the news, and are simply spiritually behind the times.

What, then, we need to know is that the Spirit has indeed been given, and that he is not a blessing to be bought, but a Gift to be received. *"Receive* ye," said Jesus as he breathed upon his diciples in the long ago. So he is saying still. This is the very heart of the Gospel. In fact it is exactly what makes a gospel of the Christian message. Jesus does not have to be coaxed into our lives. He has only, in the personality of the Holy Spirit, to be *received*. The whole New Testament fairly haunts us with this truth. "This spake he of the Spirit that they that believe on him were to *receive*. Seeing they have *received* the Holy Spirit as well as we." "Then laid they their hands on them and they *received* the Holy Spirit." And hearing this good news, Apollos believes and receives. The same rich privilege is ours also. "For this blessing is unto you and to your children and to them that are afar off, even as many as the Lord our God shall call."

We do not know as much about Apollos after this experience as we should like. But of this we may be sure, that his ministry took on a new joy and a new power. When we catch a glimpse of him in Corinth a little later we read this of him: "He helped them much." What a revealing word! When he was behind the times they spoke of him as a learned, zealous, and eloquent preacher. Now he is a helpful preacher. That is infinitely better. And the sweet wonder of it is that this is a type of ministry that is open to every one of us, whether we preach from pulpit or pew. We cannot all be learned and eloquent, but by sharing this experience of Apollos we can all be helpful. This is the sure word of Jesus himself. "If any man thirst, let him come to me, and drink. He that believeth on me, as the Scripture hath said, out of his inner life shall flow rivers of living water."

IV
MOTHER OSTRICH
(MOTHER'S DAY)

*"The daughter of my people is become cruel
like the ostriches in the wilderness."*
LAMENTATIONS 4: 3

M Y TEXT, YOU SEE, IS FROM LAMENTATIONS. IT IS
quite at home in the book of which it is a part.
It is a lament. It staggers under a weight of grief.
Every word is baptized with tears. But this text is
more than a lament. It is a sharp and cutting rebuke.
It is full of hot indignation. The prophet wields it in
honest anger, as if it were a scourge. The terrible
wrongs that are being perpetrated before his eyes, while
breaking his heart, arouse his soul to battle. He cannot look on without a protest.

I

Who is it that has thus stirred the prophet's grief
and indignation?

Strange to say, it is not some worthless father. In
those distant days, the father had quite an assured
place in the family. Of course he has lost it with the

48

passing of the years. Today he is the family joke. Here is a story that is typical: Little Johnnie had a dearly loved dog named Laddie. One day, while Johnnie was at school, Laddie got in the way of a passing car and paid the penalty. Johnnie's mother was distressed. She hardly dared tell her son of his sad loss. She thought once of telling him that the dog had strayed off. But she made up her mind that the truth must be told. So, when he came in from school, she said quite timidly: "Johnnie, Laddie was killed today." To her surprise he said, "He was?" and then went on upstairs to his play. Now, it so happened that Nurse was upstairs. She undertook to give Johnnie some details of the tragedy. At once there was a loud wail, and Johnnie came hurrying downstairs, sobbing as if his heart would break. Naturally his mother was puzzled. "Why," she asked, "are you weeping so over what Nurse said when you did not seem to mind at all when I told you that Laddie was dead?" As Johnnie struggled with his sobs, he answered, "I thought you said 'Daddy.'"

But here is a rebuke directed not against the fathers of that day, but against the mothers. Surely this prophet was quite a daring man! It takes all the courage that I can muster even to repeat his words. For this is Mother's Day. It is the day that we have set apart to honor her whose love is about the most beautiful and enriching something that this world knows. To this end we have come together, wearing red carnations for

49

the living, and white carnations for the dead. We feel deliciously sentimental. Tears are waiting just out of sight, to rush eagerly upon the scene as soon as they receive their cue. Naturally, in an atmosphere like this, these rude words of the prophet seem strikingly out of place. They jar and disappoint us. They arouse our antagonism, and leave upon our tongues a tang of the downright sacrilegious.

Now, with your resentment I have no slightest quarrel. In fact, it does you honor. It is an indication of your love and loyalty to your own mother; to her whose living presence is now perhaps your dearest joy; or whose home-going has left you your most precious memories. We all agree, I am sure, that there is no crown too resplendent to be placed upon the brow of motherhood at its best. But this prophet is daring to remind us of what we are very prone to forget on an occasion like this, and that is that motherhood in itself is not of necessity a badge of either goodness or greatness. A thoughtless, flippant, and self-centered woman is not necessarily transformed into a saint the moment she becomes a mother. There are those who remain vain, and selfish, and heartless to the end of the chapter. There are those who live and die without any realization that, in becoming mothers, one of the deepest and sweetest secrets of human blessedness has whispered itself to them, without ever being heard. It is against this type of mother that the prophet brought his bitter accusation.

II

What is the charge that he made against the mothers of that far-off day? He did not charge them with unfaithfulness to their marriage vows. He did not charge them with being mere giddy, gossiping gad-abouts. He did not accuse them of spending one half of their time at the beauty parlor and the movies and the other half at the card table. He did not accuse them of blowing cigarette smoke into the tender eyes of their babies, or of keeping them awake at night by the loud hilarity of cocktail parties. He brought against them an accusation big enough to include all these, and more. He charged them with the ugly crime of cruelty. "The daughter of my people is become cruel like the ostriches of the wilderness." Cruelty, at its best, is indifference to suffering and pain. At its worst, it is a positive delight in these.

Now, we realize at once that the crime here charged is one that is exceedingly ugly. Cruelty has never been beautiful, but it is a sin against which we of today are peculiarly hostile, especially in its cruder forms. We hate it, perhaps more than any generation that the world has ever seen. There are a good many vices that we view with indifference. There are quite a few that we have learned at once to endure, to fondle, and embrace; but cruelty is not one of them. Thanks to the Gospel of the tender Christ, the human heart has grown more sensitive with the passing of the years, till today the sight of crass cruelty makes almost all of us to burn with indignation.

For instance, in our city a few weeks ago, some men were being pestered by a mangy dog that haunted their filling station. The dog was masterless and homeless, with nobody to take his part. Therefore, partly to be rid of him, and partly out of sheer cruelty, these men dashed a bit of gasoline on him and struck a match to him. But, in spite of the fact that the dog had no master, the perpetrators of this cruel deed did not escape. The people of the community were so aroused that they had them arrested; and if I am not mistaken, they spent a few days in jail. If they did not, they deserved to do so, for they were needlessly cruel. Now, it is with the crime of cruelty that these mothers are charged, a cruelty infinitely worse than that of these thoughtless men. They are accused of being cruel to their own children.

III

What is the nature of their cruelty?

It is not the aggressive type. These mothers were not accused of inflicting any positive wrong upon their children. They were not thrusting them into some dark coal pit to do a man's work with their undeveloped bodies. They were not inflicting on them any physical harm. Had you accused them of doing so, they would have doubtless told you that they had never laid the weight of their hands upon one of their children. Their children knew nothing of kicks and cuffs. There are very few maimed bodies today because of aggressively cruel mothers. That has always been the case. These mothers of the long ago would no more have thought of inflicting positive bodily harm upon their children than the mothers of today.

What form, then, did this cruelty take? It was a cruelty, the Prophet tells, like that practiced by the ostrich. The writers of the Bible do not think highly of this bird. She is, to them, a symbol of cruelty and forgetfulness. Job describes her in this graphic fashion: "She leaveth her eggs in the earth, and warmeth them in the dust, and forgetteth that the foot may crush them, or that the wild beast may break them. She is hardened against her young ones, as though they were not hers." That is, the cruelty of the mother that so enrages the prophet is the cruelty of neglect. She cannot be bothered. She is too busy having a good time, has too many social engagements, belongs to too many clubs, to be worried by such small matters as her own children. Sometimes she is so absorbed in saving the world that she has no time for the saving of her own home.

Once, such a mother was my next-door neighbor. She never missed an opportunity to lecture on the importance of the right training of children, but she left her own largely to the nurture of the street. A cartoon of a few years ago draws her picture. A forlorn rooster is standing beside a hen's nest. The nest is

53

full of eggs that are just beginning to hatch. Some of the chicks are half out of the shell. But the hen is nowhere in sight. A friend passes and asks the rooster as to the whereabouts of his wife. As the big tears run down his face, he answers: "She's down at the Mother's Club giving a lecture on 'How to Hatch Eggs!'" This type is with us still, but thank God, she is in the minority.

IV

Why were these mothers so cruelly neglecting their children? Their neglect, I am sure, was not born of ill will. Not a mother among them ever set out deliberately to make her child a menace to himself and a menace to society. Nor was their cruelty born of utter indifference. It is a rare mother indeed who does not yearn for the best for her child. What, then, lies back of this neglect? There were doubtless a number of reasons. I am going to mention only three:

1. These mothers failed to recognize the fact that the child is of supreme value. They were, therefore, taking the fine gold of childhood, the Prophet charges, and treating it as if it were but commonplace earthenware. A recent historian has charged the downfall of Rome to the failure of her mothers. There was a time when that mother who displayed her sons as her jewels was typical of the best mothers of the empire. Those were the days of her greatness. But when they lost their sense of the supreme value of the child, then came

her days of darkness and downfall. This prophet was wise enough to know that the nation that fails to give the child first place is headed for disaster. Therefore he rebukes in words hot and passionate.

But it ought to be far harder for us to fail to set a proper valuation upon the child than for those of that far-off day. Since then Jesus has come. He is the supreme champion of the child. When his disciples asked him, "Who is greatest in the kingdom?" he did not point to any king or philosopher. He took a little child and set him in the midst. So important is the child, he tells us, that the angels that are of highest rank are the ones that have the care of children. "In heaven there angels do always behold the face of my Father." So important is the child that he solemnly warns against despising or undervaluing this treasure. "Take heed that you despise not one of these little ones." So important are they that he walls them in with a grim wall of millstones saying, "Whoso shall offend one of these little ones, it were better for him that a millstone were hanged about his neck, and that he were drowned in the depth of the sea."

But why is the child so vastly important? Of course it is important as the maker of tomorrow. Soon everything that we possess is going to slip from our nerveless fingers into the hands of our children. That is worthy of consideration. But that is not the sole secret of the child's vast importance. A child is not important because of its physical strength; it has little.

It is not important because it is a money-maker. In this respect it is a liability rather than an asset. A child is supreme, not simply because it is the highest and most intelligent of animals. Jesus put the child first because he recognized the supreme worth of the spiritual. And only as we share his convictions are we likely to join him in giving our boys and girls their place of supreme importance.

2. These mothers may have neglected their children because they failed to realize the terrible tragedy that is born of neglect. This is also true, I am sure, of a great many mothers today. Of course we recognize the deadliness of neglect in the realm of the physical. If there is a little baby in your home, you know that all you have to do to bring about the death of that baby is simply to let it alone. Neglect of its physical needs spells disaster. That we readily recognize. Not long ago a mother was executed in Germany. Her crime was this: She received a dole from the government for the support of herself and her children. But she was a pleasure-loving woman and squandered it all upon herself. The faces of her children became more and more pinched. At last they died of starvation, and this mother was arrested, tried for murder, and executed. And we feel that the sentence was just.

But our children have other hungers than those of the physical. They hunger for the Bread of Life, and thirst for the Water of Life. "The tongue of the nursing child cleaveth to the roof of his mouth for thirst,"

56

cries the indignant prophet. He knows that even children have hungers that cannot be banished by bacon and beans. Everybody ought to have wisdom enough to see that. In 1930, three thousand carefully selected leaders in child welfare met at the White House Conference for the study of the child. After the findings had been discussed, they summarized them into a Children's Charter covering nineteen points. The first was this: "For every child spiritual and moral training to help him to stand firm under the pressure of life." But that spiritual and moral training is just what is being sadly neglected today in countless homes. There are those even in the Church who, through their neglect, are rearing their children in practical paganism.

Now, the tragic cost of this cannot be estimated. I have in mind now a father and mother who are typical of all-too-many modern parents. They themselves were reared by parents who were more or less active in the Church. In their youth they attended, at least spasmodically. But now they never attend any more. Their children have never attended either Sunday school or church. On Sunday they go to the movies. They are as utterly devoid of any religious training as if their father and mother were both confirmed atheists. Yet they are the product of a so-called Christian home. And these are by no means exceptions. No wonder there is a widespread moral breakdown. Children cannot get along without religion any more than adults. A certain judge said the other day that of the more

57

than four thousands boys under twenty-one that he had sentenced, only three of them were attendants on Sunday school. How much longer will it take for us to realize the fact that our Dillingers and Clyde Barrows are not so much born as made; made by mothers and fathers guilty of the cruel sin of neglect?

3. The final reason I mention for neglect on the part of these mothers was their failure to realize the rich rewards of the mother who is willing to pay the price that real motherhood involves. There are many fine and rewarding tasks at which a mother may work, but by far the most rewarding of all is the training of her children. What are some of the rewards of the mother who, in the fear and love of God, earnestly performs this high and sacred duty?

(1) She has the reward that comes from having to give without stint, and that is the living of a full, rich life. It is costly to be a mother. "There stood by the cross of Jesus, Mary, his mother." The place of motherhood at its best is always beside the cross. Hers is a daily dying to self. But for that we should not pity her. For it is this daily dying that is the open roadway to the life abundant. If you have tears to shed, keep them for the thoughtless mother who lives for herself. The woman of all others to be envied is she who, through her daily giving, compels those who know her best to rise up and call her blessed.

(2) The second reward of the mother who is faithful to her task is that of giving to the world strong

and useful sons and daughters. Here is a mother in a hard situation. She is a slave. But one day she holds a baby to her heart that is so beautiful that, though death sentence has been pronounced against him, she simply cannot let go. "By faith Moses, when he was born, was hidden three months of his parents because they saw that he was a proper child; and they were not afraid of the king's commandment." They take a basket and line it with pitch and prayer and hide the little fellow among the rushes of the Nile. By and by in the providence of God he is back in his mother's arms again. She faithfully trains him during the few short years that he is hers. Then one day we read of him this fine word: "By faith Moses, when he was come to years, refused to be called the son of Pharaoh's daughter, choosing rather to suffer affliction with the people of God than to enjoy the pleasures of sin for a season." That was his own faith, but he had learned it at his mother's knee.

"She shot the deathless passion in her eyes
    Through him, and made him hers, and laid her mind
  On Him, and he believed in her belief."

It is to mothers such as this that humanity owes its greatest debt. It is to such that we, under God, look with hope for tomorrow.

V

A FATHER'S FAILURE
(FATHER'S DAY)

*"O my son Absalom, my son, my son Ab-
salom! would God I had died for thee, O
Absalom, my son, my son!"*
II SAMUEL 18: 33

HERE IS AN EXCEEDINGLY BITTER CRY. IT TENDS TO
make our blood run cold after all these years.
There are tears upon it that have not been dried by the
hot suns of the centuries. Who is this that is giving
way to such an abandon of grief? Surely it must be
some woman, some mother perchance, whose empty
arms are aching for the laddie that she has loved and
lost. No, that is not the case. This is not the wail of
a woman, but of a man; not of a mother, but of a father. It is King David breaking his heart over what
he regards as the greatest failure of his life.

I

Wherein has David failed? Surely his failure is not
full-orbed. In many respects he has been vastly successful. The story of his thrilling career reads like a

romance. He has come up from the ranks. Once he was only a shepherd lad with no great standing even in his own family. But he had a mind that was as brilliant as the kiss of sunlight upon clear water. He was possessed of a dauntless courage. If tradition is correct, he had the genius of a poet. While, at his worst, he was a great sinner; at his best, he was a great saint. Then he was vastly attractive. Upon all with whom he came into contact he cast a spell that was all but irresistible. Then, too, he was a practical man of affairs with his feet firmly fixed on the ground. He was a many-sided man, eminently fitted by nature to make good in any situation.

And make good he did. He climbed by rapid strides till he became king, not by right of birth, but by right of ability. As king he served his people well. He proved himself at once a great soldier and a great statesman. He soon succeeded in welding a few scattered, quarreling tribes into a compactly organized nation. He made a success financially. Much of the vast wealth that went into the building of the Temple came through his hands. In fact so wisely did he reign, that his people, throughout their subsequent history, looked back to his day as the Golden Age of Israel. Had he lived in our day we should doubtless have written a book about him entitled "From Shepherd's Tent to King's Palace." This book would certainly have found a place in "The Success Series" and have become a best seller.

In what, then, did this greatly successful man fail? He failed as a father. As a result of that failure, the body of his handsome, gifted, and favorite son is now lying, a crushed wreck in a pit in the wilderness. Therefore, while others would surely have been thrilled by the reading of David's biography, I seriously doubt if he himself could have read it with any real satisfaction. The very brilliancy of his success in certain directions must have served to give only the greater emphasis to his failure in another. As he read he would have realized that his winnings had been many and worthful. He had certainly won a secure place in the hearts of his people. But in spite of all this, the book would have left him cold. He would have been made to feel that, after all, he had majored on minors, and that his success, though very real, had been bought at too great a price.

And this is the record of so many men who are otherwise successful. I have in mind a certain gentleman who out of small beginnings succeeded in building a fortune of several millions. His brilliant success as a financier blazoned his name to the world and made him at once an object of envy and of honor. But his wealth, I am told by one who knew him well, became a weight instead of wings. It caught and held him somewhat as a piece of flypaper catches and holds a fly. In his efforts to be free, he was at times little better than a madman. Of course he had little or no time for his family. His boys grew into soft and pulpy manhood. They were far less suited to cope with their situation than their hard-working father had been to cope with his. When he died, his gold seemed to sweep over them a bit like an avalanche. They were completely swamped by their unearned wealth. Thus this father, while proving himself a conspicuous success in the building of a fortune, proved himself a yet more conspicuous failure in the building of men.

A few years ago, at one of our state fairs, a crowd was gathered about a prize hog. That hog was about all that a hog ought to be. His hair was parted in the middle and nicely combed. His hoofs were manicured in such a fashion as to have roused the envy of a movie star. Everybody who saw that hog realized that the man who raised him knew his business. Now, the boy who was set to look after this hog seemed to have been chosen as a foil to further emphasize his perfection. He was a little wizen-faced, hollow-chested, hatchet-heeled fellow who seemed bent upon burning up all the cigarettes in the world, and that as quickly as possible. He would not have walked a mile, I dare say, for his favorite brand, for he did not seem to have strength enough. He had too evidently found his unlucky strike. But the most startling fact about the whole situation was this: The father of the boy and the owner of the hog was the same man. In the hog business this father was a huge success. In the boy business he was an utter failure. And in spite of his vast abilities this also was one of the tragedies of the life of David.

II

But why does David take his failure so hard? Why is his heart so completely broken?

1. It is broken because of his deep and tender love for the son that he has lost. This I say, in spite of the fact that he was only a father. Fathers are not generally credited with doing much loving, you know. They are not supposed greatly to care. To be convinced that this is the common view, it is only necessary to contrast the celebration of Mother's Day with that of Father's Day. On the former we come together in greater numbers. We come with our largest handkerchiefs, for the atmosphere is redolent of sentiment, and we are ready at the slightest provocation to burst into tears. On Father's Day we still bring our handkerchiefs, but we use them to stifle our yawns rather than to dry our tears. However unlike the Master dad may be in other respects, he is at least like him in this, that he has made himself of no reputation.

Now, this lack of popularity is, of course, in part, his own fault, but it is not altogether so. In my opinion it is at once unfortunate and unfair. I believe, as another has suggested, that a golden halo for mother is altogether fitting. It blesses both us who give and her that receives. But I believ· also that it would be good, if we could find in our hearts to do so, to give a "little tin halo" to father now and then. It might serve to encourage him to do better. Then I ask it in the name of fair play. As I think of my own mother I think of one who was sunny and full of laughter, with never a thought of herself. As I think of my father, I think of one who was more rugged and stern, but whose unselfish devotion to his own could no more be doubted than hers. David is a father, but in spite of the fact his heart is broken over the loss of his boy.

2. Then David is crushed because his loss is without remedy. There are some mistakes that we can correct. Having blundered, we may promise ourselves to do better next time. But in many instances there is no next time. That is the tragic note in that "exceeding bitter cry" of Esau. We read that afterward when he would have inherited the blessing, he found no place for repentance. That does not mean that God refused to forgive him. It only means that he found no way of undoing the past. He could not get back into yesterday and have placed in his hands again the big opportunities that were his on life's bright morning long ago. What was done could never be undone. It is this realization that makes the grief of David all the more bitter. He is facing the fact that of the things that have no next time, one, at least, is the rearing of a son. How many things he now feels that he could do for Absalom were he only a little boy again! But that can never be. Therefore, there is the agony of utter

65

hopelessness in his cry, "O my son Absalom, O my son, my son Absalom! would God I had died for thee!"

3. But the note of supreme bitterness in the sorrow of David, that which brings his grief to its tragic climax, is the haunting fear that the boy that he has lost hopelessly he has also lost needlessly. He has lost him when he might have saved him. "Had I only been a better father to him, had I only acted differently," he keeps telling his tortured soul, "then he would be with me now instead of yonder in the pit, under the stones. I have lost him and it's all my fault." This is the nagging fear that becomes a conviction that he cannot shake off. It is a conviction that bites like a serpent and stings like an adder. His loss would have been hard enough if he could have persuaded himself that he had done his best. But this he cannot do. His hell is that such a persuasion is impossible.

One day in Texas a farmer was in the field plowing cotton. With him were his two small boys. He looked up from his task to see a large dog coming toward them. This dog was snapping at the cotton stalks, and the farmer saw that he was mad. At once he put himself between his boys and the dog. He told them to run for refuge to a nearby cotton bin, while he kept the dog away. The boys made good their escape. But not so the father. He was forced to fight the dog, and that with no weapon but his pocket knife. As a result he was bitten from his face to his feet. Medical science could do nothing for him. But during his lucid intervals, as death crept upon him, he would look into the face of his wife with a smile and say, "Don't you worry about me. I saved our boys." And he went out to meet God unafraid. I think he could have done so, even if the boys had died with him, seeing that he did his best. But to lose when we might have done better, that is "sorrow's crown of sorrow." And that is the pathetic plight of David. He has lost his son—lost him hopelessly, and lost him needlessly.

III

How did David come to make this terrible failure?

He did not do so, I am sure, because Absalom was born a traitor. He was born with a capacity for treachery, but he was also born with a capacity for faithfulness and loyalty. "What manner of child shall this be?" was asked by a group who stood about the cradle of John the Baptist. Is there any sure answer to such a question? The Catholic Church has always believed that there is. As it looks into the face of a little child, it says without hesitation, "This child will be a Catholic." The Jews believe that there is an answer to that question. As they look into the face of a baby, they do not hesitate to say, "This child will be a Jew." But Protestantism is often far less sure. That is one of our chief weaknesses. Too often we answer, "The Lord only knows!" And then hurry about our business or pleasure. Yet both the Scriptures and experience teach that if we train a child in the way he shall go, when he is old, he will not depart from it.

If, then, David did not fail because failure was inevitable, why, I repeat, did he fail? There are, I think, two outstanding reasons.

1. He failed because he shifted the responsibility for the care of his son upon the shoulders of others instead of taking it upon himself. What he did in this last scene is, I think, typical of his entire relationship to Absalom. When his soldiers were going out to battle, a battle that was to determine whether he himself was to keep his crown and his life, it was not of these that he was thinking. He was thinking only of his loved and treacherous son. "Deal gently for my sake," he told his officers in the presence of the army. "Deal gently, for my sake, with the young man, Absalom." But when the army had marched out of sight, he was doubtless very uneasy. "My officers are good and loyal men," he probably kept telling himself. "Still I am greatly afraid for my son. I should have gone myself. Yes, at all costs I should have made the safety of my boy a personal matter."

But who is that coming across the plain? It is a messenger. The king is all solicitude, but his anxiety is only for his son. "Victory!" the messenger shouts through panting lips. But the father has no ear for such a message. There is but one question, "Is the young man Absalom safe?" The first messenger did not have the heart to tell, but yonder comes another,

"Victory!" he shouts also. But David asks that same eager, anxious question, "Is the young man Absalom safe?" Then comes the tragic answer, and David is a broken old man. "O my son Absalom," he sobs, "I am so sorry now that I did not go out even at the cost of my life. Better a million times that I should be lying under the stones than you."

Now, what David did in this instance, I repeat, he has done through the years. It is true that he has a good excuse for his conduct. We are in no sense disposed to judge him harshly. He has been a man of many cares. He has been burdened by matters of state. Naturally he has not had much time for his children. But we cannot shut our eyes to the pathos of it all. For, as a result, he never really got acquainted with Absalom, never gained his confidence, never won his heart. In his younger years, when he had a broken toy, Absalom never thought of going to his father about it. Nor did he think of doing so in later years when he had a broken heart. Father and son were both most fascinating, but they never became friends. And yet David gave Absalom everything except himself. But failing to give himself, he failed altogether. Thus he lost a treasure far more priceless than his crown.

How David would have envied the humble father of whom his son could say this:

> "He's the best thing, daddy is,
> When he ain't got the rheumatiz,

Gives me pennies and good advice,
'Bout keeping clean and being nice,
Saying please, and don't deceive,
Handkerchief, instead of sleeve.
Seems just like 'at daddy knew,
He was once a small boy, too.
Second table for him, I spec,
With nothing but the chicken neck.
Anyhow he always says,
Give the kid the best there is.
And when Ma sends me off to bed,
He always takes the light ahead,
And holds my hand and talks maybe,
About the things that used to be,
When he and Uncle was little boys,
And all about their games and toys,
What am I gonner be, Gee whiz,
I'm gonner be like daddy is.
I'd rather be like him, 'ijing,
Than president or anything.
He's like Ma says angels is
When he ain't got the rheumatiz."

But David was too busy. As so many today, he "passed the buck," lost his boy, and broke his own heart.

2. The second reason for David's falure was his bad example. There was a time, after he had become a father, that he allowed himself a most tragic visit to the far country. He became a prodigal. In utter disregard to his obligations to others, he took a woman to whom he had no right. Later he murdered her husband to conceal his crime. No wonder that when his

oldest son wanted a woman for himself, he took her ruthlessly, even though she was his half sister. Had not his father set him the example? And that father, having done so, dared not punish his brutal son. Thus Absalom felt called upon to take vengeance into his own hands and punish his brother. All this brought an ever-widening chasm between himself and his father until it ended in utter tragedy. No wonder, therefore, that David felt, and rightly so, that he had the blood of his ruined boy on his own hands. He had employed two most effective methods of destruction, a bad example and neglect.

But, you answer, was not David a good man? Yes, David repented of his terrible sin and God in his mercy forgave him. But, while David's repentance brought him personal salvation, it did not bring salvation to his wayward boy. David made one excursion into the far country, and Absalom followed his steps; but when David came back, so far as this son was concerned, he came back alone. That is a tragedy that has happened times without number. Years ago I had a neighbor who was the father of a large family. He was a drinking man, though not a drunkard. He was friendly toward religion, though he seldom went to church. But when he was between fifty and sixty years of age, he was soundly and happily converted. How hard he tried to atone for his wasted years! How eager he was to reach his children, all of whom had now grown to manhood and womanhood! I have seen him stand up in the little village church to read a bit, only to burst into tears. But his children were not softened by these tears—they were only shamed by them. They went with him into the far country, but the poor broken father came back alone. May God save us from such a tragedy! That he may do so, let us as parents in the fear of God take the responsibility for the welfare of our children upon ourselves.

VI

THE GREAT ESSENTIAL
(COMMENCEMENT DAY)

"By faith, they [the Israelites] passed through the Red sea as by dry land: which the Egyptians assaying to do were swallowed up."

HEBREWS 11: 29

HERE IS A STORY OUT OF A DISTANT YESTERDAY. Two groups, the Israelites and the Egyptians, journeyed down the same road. They took the same turnings. They were lighted by the same sun. They came to the same obstacle, the same seemingly impossible barrier. They came to the Red Sea. They both undertook to cross this sea. But here their likeness ends. The outcome of their adventure was by no means the same. For the Egyptians, the undertaking ended in disaster; while for the Israelites, it ended in victory. One found the Red Sea a terminus; the other found it a thoroughfare. One found it a roadway to death; while the other found it a roadway to life. On the next day, the Israelities were shouting the praises of God on the further shore, while the bodies of the Egyptians were being spit out upon that same shore by a nauseated sea.

Why was this the case? It was certainly not because of any superiority of culture and equipment on the part of these Jews. They were a horde of slaves. The Egyptians, on the other hand, were a proud and conquering people. Nor were the differing issues of their adventure due to the fact that these Israelities were the especial favorites of Heaven. God does not play favorites. If my house is dark this morning while yours is flooded with light, it is not because the sun has a prejudice against me and a fondness for you. It is because you have opened the blinds and given the sun a chance, while I have refused to do so. If your life is lighted by the Sun of Righteousness, while mine is in darkness, it is not because he is a respecter of persons. It is rather because you have by your attitude made this illumination possible, while I have made it impossible.

Why, then, I repeat, did the Israelites succeed while the Egyptians failed? It was not because of an outward, but because of an inward difference. The Egyptians came to this crisis without faith in God. They were simply out in pursuit of a horde of runaway slaves. They were out with no higher purpose than the recovery of their property. The Israelites, on the other hand, were making an adventure of faith. It was not a perfect faith. That was not necessary. If we have genuine faith to any degree, even as a grain of mustard seed, it becomes a power in our lives that enables us to do the impossible. The man possessing it,

74

says Jesus, can toss mountains about as a juggler tosses a ball.

I

Now, young gentlemen, this story may be old beyond your interest. Coming out of that far-gone yesterday, it may seem removed by millions of leagues from the perplexing time in which your lot is cast. Yet if some man of genius were today to give himself to the task of writing a story that would exactly fit into our present needs, I am not sure that he could improve on this one. Ours is a day of vast bewilderment. For some, old foundations have given away, old convictions broken down. Many have become cynical, embittered, disillusioned. Many have lost faith in God, faith in themselves, faith in any real purpose for the life that now is. What has this ancient writer to say to us in our bewilderment?

He ventures to tell us that what we need most is faith in God. Faith, he asserts, is not a mere elective in the school of life, it is a requirement; not a luxury, but an absolute necessity. He dares to assert that the difference between real success and utter failure, between victory and defeat, triumph and tragedy, is a matter of faith. He affirms that, when we come to the difficult crossings of life, that which will determine whether we shall win over or go down will not be our native ability, nor our skill and culture, nor some lucky break, but our faith in God. It is his conviction

75

that faith is the one absolute essential in the business of living.

Now, while there are those who deny the necessity of religious faith, none can deny the necessity of faith in general. Some sort of faith is absolutely essential to the carrying on of the everyday business of life. "Without faith," says this writer, "it is impossible to please God." We might without violence leave off the latter half of the sentence, and read, "Without faith it is impossible." What is impossible? Every really constructive and worth-while something. We must have faith in order to do as commonplace thing as drive a car. It takes faith to press the starter. If you do not believe that such a foolish-looking procedure will set the motor in motion you are likely to refuse to "step on it." It takes even a greater faith to drive at the rate of sixty miles an hour over a road that you have never traveled before. It requires faith to mail a letter. What a foolish procedure it seems to intrust an important document to a little iron box fixed to a post! Then, faith is absolutely essential to the carrying on of the commerce of the world. Every store, every bank would fail without it. Faith is essential to the work of the scientist. Unless he believes that this is an ordered universe he will make no progress. It is on faith that every real home is builded. And no home will last for an hour after faith is dead.

But faith in God is just as essential as is faith on the

lower levels of life. This is true for at least two reasons:

1. Nothing really counts without it. Were it possible for one to possess all else, but have no faith in God, the business of living must be for that one nothing more than a sheer futility. This fact has been demonstrated by actual experience times without number. Take the case of Hamlet, Prince of Denmark, for instance. He was a man of fine abilities. He had a royal stage upon which to use these abilities. True, his situation bristled with difficulties. But these might have been his opportunities. True, the times were out of joint, but that gave him the big chance of setting them right. But what did he do with this situation that was so rich in possibilities? He made an utter mess of it all. He could find no finer task in the face of his nation's need than to play with the idea of suicide. He did not take the final plunge, but that which kept him from it was not any high sense of duty, nor any solid conviction; it was rather a sickening fear that he might find the afterlife worse than the present.

> "Who would fardels bear,
> To grunt and sweat under a weary life,
> But that the dread of something after death—
> The undiscover'd country, from whose bourn
> No traveller returns,—puzzles the will,
> And makes us rather bear those ills we have
> Than fly to others that we know not of."

He was richly endowed, but, wanting faith, he counted for nothing in setting the wrongs of his nation right.

The hero of "Invictus" was certainly a courageous soul. It is impossible not to admire him for his rugged strength. There is no hint of weakness in his valiant song:

> "Out of the night that covers me,
>   Black as the pit from pole to pole,
> I thank whatever gods may be,
>   For my unconquerable soul.

> "In the fell clutch of circumstance,
>   I have not winced nor cried aloud,
> Under the bludgeonings of chance,
>   My head is bloody, but unbowed.

> "Beyond this world of griefs and tears,
>   Looms but the horror of the shade,
> And yet the menace of the years,
>   Finds and shall find me unafraid.

> "It matters not how straight the gate,
>   How charged with punishments the scroll,
> I am the master of my fate,
>   I am the captain of my soul."

But what does all his splendid courage do for him? Nothing better than this—it leaves him under a sky that is black as the pit from pole to pole. It leaves him, also, facing a future without hope, for in the morrow there looms nothing better than the horror of the shade. In spite of his heroic courage, therefore, lacking faith, life for him is the grimmest of tragedies.

The preacher in Ecclesiastes is so richly endowed that he seems to possess almost everything. He has material wealth. He has vast power. He has ability to the point of genius. He used his immense resources to experiment in the business of living. He tries pleasure. He tries achievement. He tries wisdom. But all his efforts at rich and joyful living end in disaster. "I hated life," he confesses, disgustedly. "Vanity of vanities!" he spits from his lips like dry ashes. What is the matter? It is not that life has wrenched all worldly treasure from his hands and flung him aside to die in shame. His cry of disillusionment is rather the cry of one into whose roomy hands life has dumped every gift except the supreme gift of faith. He has no faith, and wanting that, he wants all else of real value. Faith, therefore, is essential because all wealth without it leaves its possessor poverty-stricken.

2. Then, faith in God is the great essential because if we possess it, however great our poverty in other directions, we are still rich. The truth is that nothing can really defeat us if we keep a firm faith in God. Life certainly deals far more harshly with some than with others. But it is not what life does to us that determines our triumph or tragedy. It is not the heavy blows that are dealt us that are the deciding factors in our victory or defeat. It is our reaction to these blows. And what that reaction is depends largely upon our

faith. Paul discovered the truth of this in his own experience. It had cost him much to be a Christian. He tells us frankly that he has had to suffer the loss of all things. But he affirms that these losses have not impoverished him, but have made him vastly richer. And what he has found true in his own experience he is sure will be true for all of us. "We know," he declares, "that all things work together for good to them that love God." Faith, therefore, is the great essential because if we possess it real failure is impossible.

II

Why is this the case?

There is no magic about it. Nor is it true because faith in God exempts its possessor from "the slings and arrows of outrageous fortune." Such is not the case. God's flowers are not hothouse plants. To suppose that by believing in God we can avoid all life's rough places is to be disappointed. In the old-time Sunday school stories there was usually a good boy set in marked contrast to a bad boy. The contrast usually consisted in this: The good boy was always reaching in his thumb and pulling out a plum, while the bad one was coming out the little end of the horn. But life soon dynamites that complacent theory. As we look about us we are impressed by "the broad sameness of the human lot." Whether believers or unbelievers, we all come to our Red Seas. We all meet difficulties. Bad men sometimes go broke, and good men do the same. Bad men and good men lose their health. Bad men and good men bury their loved ones. The good of faith, therefore, is not that it gives its possessor exemption from the conflicts that are inevitable in a world like ours, but rather that it brings inward strength to triumph over them. It energizes our hearts with the power of Him of whom it is written, "He shall not fail nor be discouraged."

Illustrations of the truthfulness of this abound on every hand. I have in mind two men who recently suffered heavy financial losses. One of them still had enough left to have kept him in comfort for a lifetime, while the other was so reduced as to be forced to accept charity. How did they meet this difficult crossing? The one who had lost only a part of his fortune locked himself in his room and took his own life. But the other is living today more abundantly than ever before. He is even able to thank God for that which he once thought must work his ruin. Thus he passed through his Red Sea as by dry land, which the other assaying to do was swallowed up.

Such stories could be duplicated in almost every community. During the past three years more than sixty thousand people in the United States have flung out of life by suicide. Many of these were hard hit. They were face to face with dire tragedy. Some had lost their wealth. Some had lost their health. Some had seemingly lost their very all. But this does not fully explain their failure. They were no worse off than many thousands of their fellows who are today carrying on and facing up to their situations with quiet hearts and steady eyes. Their real tragedy was that they became bankrupt in faith. A man may live on very little if he has much to live for. But the wealth of the world is not enough to live on when there is nothing left to live for. That which gives us something to live for is faith.

Not long ago I had two members of my church who were compelled to consult a physician. Upon both of them the physician passed sentence of death. He told them that they were suffering from the same type of incurable disease. One, a brilliant young physician, hurried to his office and blew his brains out. The other faced her heavy ordeal with a calm courage that made her a blessing to everyone that came in contact with her. Here again, the possessor of faith won her way to the shores of victory, while the other assaying the same difficult crossing was drowned. Thus does human experience constantly join its voice to the Apostle in declaring: "This is the victory that overcometh the world, even our faith."

III

Now, assuming that you agree with the author of this text regarding the importance of faith—how are we to come into possession of such a treasure?

In our search there are a few beaten tracks that we shall do well to avoid. For instance, we are not going to arrive by constantly magnifying and talking up our doubts. A very wise man said recently that we talk our way into unbelief far more often than we think our way there. Nor are we likely to arrive by regarding our doubts as assets rather than liabilities. "The fool has said in his heart, there is no God." The trouble with this fool is not in his head, but in his heart. Having dismissed God, he heaves a huge sigh of relief. He has thus relieved himself from weighty responsibilities that he does not wish to meet. He has thus been enabled to descend from mountain heights where breathing was a bit difficult into a lotus land where he can relax. Of course no one who clings to his doubts because of an enervating fear of that which is high and exacting will ever come to a vital faith. No more will he who waits for the answer to all his questions. There will always be veils through which we cannot see, and doors to which we find no key. But this need not prove our undoing, for faith is essentially an adventure.

How, then, are we going to win? The process may be long and difficult, but the first step is plain. We must begin here and now to live up to the best that we know. However little we may believe, however far we may be from a living faith, if we have the will to believe that expresses itself in obedience to the highest that we know, that is enough for a beginning. For the man who dares to live up to the light that he has will surely come to a fuller light. This is the explicit declaration of Jesus himself: "If any man is willing to do his will, he shall know." It is, also, the experience of an innumerable company that have tested it in their own lives. Let us dare to put it to the test, and we, too, shall come into possession of that rare treasure that will enable us to pass through our Red Seas as by dry land.

VII

THE FORGOTTEN DAY

(SABBATH OBSERVANCE DAY)

"The sabbath was made for man, and not man for the sabbath."

MARK 2: 27

I DESIRE TO THINK WITH YOU OF OUR CHRISTIAN Sabbath. That we are a long way from the Sabbath of our fathers is evident to the most superficial observer. For this some are devoutly thankful. They look back upon the Sundays of yesterday with a kind of horror. With a swagger of superiority they speak of them as "blue Sundays." However, I am quite sure that they were not vastly blue to those who lived through them. Speaking out of my own experience, my boyhood Sundays were anything but blue. There was a joyfulness about the day that belonged to no other day in the week. On Sunday we wore our best clothes and enjoyed our best dinners. On that day the sun seemed to shine a bit brighter, and the birds to sing a bit sweeter. On that day the church bell, as it called the people to worship, had in its deep tones a note of healing, as of celestial music.

Today all this is changed. Whatever may be the color of our present Sunday, it is certainly not blue. It seems rather to be a glaring scarlet. For this once restful day is now set aside for our most hectic and exciting pleasures. It is a day of open theaters and of open shops. It is a day of commercialized amusement. It is a day when vast numbers of our fellows must not only work, but work under extra pressure. It is a day when our roads are most congested by cars, when accidents are most numerous, when our hospitals receive their largest number of wounded, and our undertaking establishments their largest number of dead. No, the day is certainly not blue, but scarlet, save where it is flecked by bits of white, due to the presence in an unusual degree of the pale horse and his rider.

Now, in the language of the street, "How have we got that way?" This change has not come about, I am sure, because of any deeper appreciation on our part of the values that are spiritual. It is certainly not the result of a revival of vital religion. No more is it the result of a fuller investigation of the Scriptures, and of a deeper exploring of the mind of Christ. In truth I am sure that this change has not come about under the leadership of the Church at all. The Church has rather been caught by the strong currents of the world, till churched and unchurched have largely lost this once holy day out of their lives. We have not so much thought our way to this change as we have drifted into it under the spell of the worship of the twin gods of pleasure and gold.

Therefore it seems to me that it would be vastly wise for us who call ourselves Christians to stop taking our cue from the world and to seek the mind of Christ on this important matter. When we turn to the New Testament what do we find? The answer will seem to some at once surprising and disappointing. We learn that Jesus gives no specific command regarding the observance of the Christian Sabbath. The early Christians began to observe the day in remembrance of the Resurrection. Three centuries later, under Constantine, it became a legal holiday. Sunday, therefore, as we know it, is a gift of the Church. But that does not discount it. The same is the case with the New Testament. The New Testament did not make the Church; the Church made the New Testament. We believe that it gave this Testament, under the leadership of the Spirit. We may believe, also, that the Church was Spirit-guided in giving us the Christian Sabbath. But it is evident that the concern of Jesus is not whether we observe the first or the seventh day. He is only concerned that we observe one day in seven. That he gives his sanction to this is clearly taught in our text, "The sabbath was made for man, and not man for the sabbath."

I

What does Jesus mean by this?

1. He means that the Sabbath is God's gift to man.

He gives it to him as he gives him countless other gifts. "Every good gift and every perfect gift is from above, and cometh down from the Father of lights with whom is no variableness, neither shadow cast by turning." He gives it to him as he gives him this lovely world with its mountains and hills, with its blooming flowers and singing birds, with its rippling streams and rolling rivers. God gives man the Sabbath in love because he knows that man needs it.

2. Not only is the Sabbath made for man, but it is made for the whole man. Man needs the Sabbath physically. He can do more work on six days than he can in seven. Not only so, but he needs the Sabbath morally and spiritually. It is his opportunity to recover his poise, to tone up his life, to open the windows of his soul out toward the heavenly Jerusalem. It is not only an opportunity to receive, but also to give. The whole man needs the Sabbath.

3. Since God gives the Sabbath to man, he does not give it simply to one man, nor to a certain type of man, but to all men of all times. He gives it to all, because it is needed by all. In fact if it was needed in the long ago, that need has become more intense with the passing of the years. The Sabbath, therefore, is for all men. It is made for the man who toils with his hands and the man who toils with his brain. It is made for the ice man. Therefore, we ought, so far as possible, to refrain from buying ice on Sunday. It is meant for the man at the filling station. Therefore, we ought not

to take it away from him. It is meant for professional athletes and for theatrical folks. Therefore, we have no right to wrench this gift out of their hands by compelling them to work on Sunday. It is made even for "soda jerkers" and caddies. Every man has a right to a Sabbath.

4. It is God's gift to man as a group. He needs it as a nation. He needs it as a world. The nation that observes the Sabbath has a moral stability and healthy-mindedness that the nation that ignores it does not have. In fact we can measure the religious prosperity of a nation very largely by its observance of the Sabbath. The nation that ignores the Sabbath and secularizes it is on the way to losing its religion and thus to losing its soul. The Sabbath, therefore, is God's good gift to man. Its right use surely makes for the highest good both of the individual and of society as a whole.

II

Now, it is possible for us to refuse this gift of the Sabbath, and thereby allow all its values to be lost. The fact that God has given us the Sabbath does not mean that we have to accept it. We do not have to accept any gift from God or man. We speak of giving our children an education, but that we cannot do. We can give them an opportunity at an education, but if they do not receive the gift, we are powerless. God can offer us the gift of Eternal Life, but if we do not take it, it will never be ours. The same is true of the gift of the Sabbath. It is ours for the taking, but we may refuse to accept it and thereby lose it.

For multitudes of us today, both within the Church and without, the Sabbath is largely a lost gift. We have lost it by simply leaving it alone. For, in order to lose our Sabbath we do not have to preach against it; we do not have to repeal all laws regarding it; all we have to do is to treat it as we treat any other day. "The Sabbath was made for man." If this is true, then to claim that this Sabbath is to be used just as we use every other day is to accuse Jesus of talking nonsense. If we do not use the Sabbath in a different fashion from that in which we use other days, then we are refusing to accept God's good gift.

Of course I am aware of the arguments against this. We say that every day ought to be holy unto the Lord. And that is true. But the man who observes the Sabbath is far more likely to observe the other days as holy than the man who does not. The same argument is used against going to church, "Every place," we claim, "ought to be a holy place." Yet the man who has no special place for worship is very likely not to find a holy place anywhere. To treat the Sabbath, therefore, as we treat every other day is to lose it, and in losing it to help rob ourselves and our fellows as well.

III

Then it is possible to misuse this gift. That is true of all gifts. An automobile is a thing of value. The other day a father gave his son a beautiful new one. He gave it to him because he loved him and because he wished to give him pleasure. But the son took that car and tried to climb a telephone pole with it and thus ended in the hospital. The fault was not with the car. It was with the use that the son made of it. Money is good. It is a blessing, if rightly used. But it may become a curse. The same is true of the gifts of physical charm and beauty. It is also true of great intellectual gifts. In fact there is no treasure that God puts into our hands that we have not the power to misuse.

1. Some misuse the Sabbath by putting it to uses that are, to say the least, of secondary value. There are those, for instance, who go into a comatose state every Sunday. They sleep and idle all day. There are others who grunt all day Sunday. I used to have a woman in my church who enjoyed good health all through the week, but on Sunday she enjoyed bad health. She had seventh-day headaches that were something terrible. Then there are those who play all day Sunday. They make it not a holy day, but a holiday only. Now this is better doubtless than utter neglect, but it is only a second best.

2. Then some misuse the day by making it an end in itself. This was what the Pharisees were doing in the days of Jesus. They had somehow reached the conclusion that man was made for the Sabbath, not the Sabbath for man. Believing this, they constantly

91

sought to fit man into the needs of the Sabbath instead of the Sabbath into the needs of man. Therefore they hedged the day about by many restrictions. It became a day of repression rather than a day of expression, a day of "don'ts" rather than a day of "dos." There were so many petty things that were forbidden on the Sabbath that it took a learned man to know them all. For instance, if one were bitten by a flea on the Sabbath he was not allowed to catch and exterminate the pest lest he should be guilty of desecrating the holy day by hunting. Thus they changed the day, for many, from a blessing into a burden. The same was true of the strictest of the Puritans. The same is true of some very earnest people in our own day.

Now the attitude of Jesus was vastly different. He believed in the Sabbath just as genuinely as the most rigid of the Pharisees or Puritans. But he believed in it as a means to an end, and not as an end in itself. To him the supreme values were always human values. He determined the worth of every institution by one test, its power to serve and enrich the whole life of man. Putting this test to the Sabbath, he used it in a fashion that seemed to the Pharisees outrageous and wicked. Believing that the Sabbath was made for man, he constantly used it for man. In fact it was this courageous putting of human values first on the part of Jesus that did more than anything else to dig a chasm between himself and the religious leaders of his day and to send him at last to the cross.

Take this scene, for example. One Sabbath day Jesus came upon a man who had been sick for thirty and eight years. This man had lost hope. He had no expectation of the dawn of a tomorrow. But Jesus said, "Arise, take up thy bed, and walk." The man at once got upon his feet and took up his bed and went his way. When certain Jews saw him carrying his bed, they rebuked him for thus desecrating the Sabbath. But the healed man gave the wise answer: "The Man that cured me told me to carry my bed." Now, the logical question would have been, "Who healed you?" But that, they did not ask. They only asked, "Who told you to carry your bed?" They were not interested in the remaking of this man. They were only interested in the keeping of the Sabbath. Thus they misused the day by putting institutional values above human values.

And mark you, this wrong sense of values continues to work tragedy to this day, not only with regard to our use of the Sabbath, but of other institutions as well. We are still too often like the dentist who, having made for a patient a pair of teeth that did not fit, sought to adjust the mouth of the patient to the teeth instead of the teeth to the mouth of the patient. We still tend to believe that man was made for the factory instead of the factory for the man; that man was made for the state instead of the state for man. Sometimes we even persuade ourselves that man was made for the Church instead of the Church for man. But no institution, either secular or religious, has a right to exist save as it builds up and conserves human values. "The Sabbath was made for man, and not man for the Sabbath."

IV

What, then, are we to do with our Sabbath? How are we to observe it?

There are many who would like some specific and definite rules, such as "do this" and "don't do that." But we find no such in the New Testament. Jesus never gave rules. A rule may be timely, but it is never timeless. A rule that fits one situation would not fit another. But while Jesus gave no rules, he did lay down great principles. And principles are both timely and timeless. For instance, though Palestine was a part of a great empire the majority of whose population were slaves, Jesus never said a word against human slavery. But he did say, "All things whatsoever ye would that men should do to you, do ye even so to them." He never said a word against child labor, but he did say, "It were better to have a great millstone hung about your neck, and be drowned in the depths of the sea, than to offend one of these little ones that believe in me." He never said a word against the liquor traffic, but he did say, "Thou shall love thy neighbor as thyself." He gave no specific rules for the keeping of the Sabbath. But he did say that it was made for man, that it was, therefore, to be used for man's highest good.

Suppose you and I were to begin here and now to

live up to that. Certain obvious results would surely follow. We should seek always to act in such a fashion as to make it possible for every man to appropriate this Sabbath that was made for his benefit. We should, therefore, refuse to compel any man to do unnecessary work on the Sabbath either for our pleasure or for our financial gain. This in itself would put an end to almost all our buying and selling. It would also close up all places of commercialized amusement. Of course the usual answer to this is, "If I don't rob the other fellow of his Sabbath by patronizing him, somebody else will!" That, too, is the answer of the bootlegger, "Men are going to have liquor. If I don't sell it, somebody else will." Then, let them. "It must needs be," said Jesus, "that offenses come; but woe to that man by whom the offense cometh." But acting on this principle we shall do more than simply refusing to rob others, we shall seek to enrich them by doing positive good on the Sabbath. Though our circumstances are vastly different from those of Jesus, it might be instructive to ask how he used this day. When we turn to the record we find that he made at least three definite uses of the Sabbath.

1. He used it for fellowship with his friends. When invited, he went into their homes and took dinner with them. He walked abroad with them. It is a good day still for innocent recreation, for families to reunite, and for friends to get together in wholesome fellowship.

2. Jesus made the Sabbath a day of worship. Luke

95

tells us that he made a habit of going to church on that day. The church of his day was not conspicuous for its spirituality. It was rather cold and lifeless. But Jesus knew that he would not remedy its defects by merely leaving it alone. He sought to help by attending its service. I believe we should find it helpful to follow his example. Sunday gives us an opportunity to withdraw from the world, and in the fellowship of our brethren, to worship God.

3. Jesus used the Sabbath as a day for helping others. It gave him some of his best opportunities to teach and heal. Here, too, we might do well to follow his example. Many of us are too busy during the week to have much time for definite service of others. Often our time is not our own. But Sunday offers us this opportunity. On that day, in an especial sense, it is our privilege to forget ourselves in the service of our fellows. But no one can lay down exact rules for another. The broad principle is this: Refuse to use the day selfishly in the service of pleasure and gold, and use it unselfishly in the service of man and God, and that is enough. If those in America who belong to the Church were to begin today to treat the Sabbath in this fashion, I am confident that they themselves would be vastly enriched, and our whole nation would soon be led into a new day of spiritual life and power.

VIII

THE WORK OF THE EVANGELIST
(EVANGELISM)

"Do the work of an evangelist"
II TIMOTHY 4: 5

I

EVANGELISM IS A BEAUTIFUL WORD THAT HAS LOST its winsomeness. Somehow in its journey from the Jerusalem of yesterday to the Jericho of today it has fallen among thieves that have wounded it and stripped it, and departed, leaving it half dead. It takes a rather rash Samaritan, therefore, to dare turn aside to set this poor chap upon his beast and take him to an inn and take care of him. This is especially true because a veritable procession of priests and Levites are passing by, not only refusing to lend a hand, but, we fear, inwardly chuckling at the plight of the poor fellow, and secretly hoping that they are soon to see the last of him.

Now, this has not always been the case. I am not among the ancients, but I can remember when the first day of the revival brought the people together in unusual numbers and with heightened expectancy. And

97

I have seen multitudes come together greatly wondering, saying, "What do these things mean?" because there were big events taking place that could only be accounted for in terms of God. But that is largely of yesterday. The announcement of a revival in the average church is no longer a clarion call for the rallying of the hosts of Zion. It is rather a warning gong that calls, "To your tents, O Israel." Our people, even some of the best, flee for refuge to the security of their homes, or to their cars on the open road. The announcement of a revival today in the average city church would be about as effective in bringing together a congregation as if the pastor were to say, "My brethren, next Sunday we are to have on exhibition in this church some very interesting cases of contagious disease. If you come and bring your families, you may be able to contract one or more of them."

As to just how this change has come about, it is not my purpose fully to explain. Of course I know the one on whose shoulders we are accustomed to lay the heaviest part of the responsibility. It is upon the professional evangelist. But, of course, no fair-minded man would make a wholesale condemnation of these ministers. Some of them are the salt of the earth. They are holy men, the latches of whose shoes I personally feel myself unworthy to unloose. But there was a type of which this is not the case. You remember how they used to come with their high-powered methods and their veteran sermons that had done yeoman service in many a hard-fought campaign, but had not grown shorter, but rather longer. For you know an old sermon is a bit like a snowball rolling down a hill—it grows larger all the time, but what it accumulates is generally rubbish. These brethren often had a genius for counting sham results and real money. They reigned as kings for a few days, and then folded their tents like the Arabs, and silently went away, leaving us on four flat tires spiritually, and with our spares stolen.

But even for this type of spurious evangelism the evangelist was by no means solely to blame. An equal if not a heavier part of the responsibility must be put upon the pastor and his people. Often when we invited the evangelist we did not do so because we were eager for a real refreshing from the presence of the Lord. We were rather seeking a smooth road out of a hard situation. We wanted a million-dollar return on a five-cent investment. We were eager for a bumper crop without giving ourselves to the prosaic task of clearing and breaking and tilling the soil. This counterfeit evangelism, I am sure, has done much to bring the genuine into disrepute.

Then, there are those who look askance at evangelism, because they feel that it has been too individualistic, and has demanded too small a sovereignty over life. But in my opinion, our lost passion for evangelism is due more to our lost sense of God than to any other cause. "Then," said I, "here am I, send me," is the testimony of one who years ago burned with a hot enthusiasm for sharing the blessings that had come into his own life. "Then," this is a backward-looking word. Upon what does it look? It looks back to the time when Isaiah had seen "the Lord high and lifted up"; to the time when in the light of that vision he had seen himself as a sinner, and had been made clean. The fires of evangelism always burn in hearts that are conscious of the Divine Presence. And when men lose that consciousness, the fires go out.

II

Just what do we mean by evangelism? Its simplest meaning, as you know, is to tell Good News. But fully to understand it we need more than a definition—we need to see it in terms of personality. Let us, therefore, turn to the Supreme Evangelist. Mark, in his romantic and aggressive gospel, shows Him to us with peculiar clearness. "And Jesus came into Galilee preaching the Good News about God." He told men that they were all the sons of God, that it was every man's privilege to call God "Father." He showed how life's supreme tragedy consists in our effort to be independent toward our Father. That was the tragedy of the graceless laddie of whom we read in the fifteenth chapter of St. Luke. He went away from home, not because he wanted to grieve his father, but because he wanted to be independent of him. But life was transfigured for him the moment he determined to take a son's place in his father's house.

By telling men that they are all the sons of God, he told them the further "Good News" that they were brothers one to the other. He told them that no man need live as a stranger in this world, that men need no longer glare at each other across frozen chasms of indifference, or fiery chasms of hate—that every man might see in his fellow a brother. And Jesus not only preached brotherhood, but he lived it. He put himself under every man's load. He dined with outcasts. He talked to harlots with the same gracious courtesy that he showed to the purest of the pure. Thus he dug a chasm between himself and decent folks and went to the cross for doing the work of an evangelist.

But after Jesus had been crucified, men who had been baptized into his spirit took up his message. One gifted young man, by the name of Stephen, evangelized so compellingly in Jerusalem that "they were not able to resist the spirit and the wisdom by which he spake." Unable to answer him with words, they mobbed him. But though they stoned the life from his body, they could not stone the radiance from his face, "They saw his face as if it had been the face of an angel." Though they robbed him of his life, they could not rob him of his love. He died with this Christlike prayer upon his lips: "Lord, lay not this sin to their charge."

Among those having a part in this ghastly crime was a young man who was about the best intellect of his day. He tried to forget the ugly memory by giving himself to an orgy of persecution. But he was never able to brush the beauty of that radiant face from his mind. He was never able to stop his ears to that Christ-like prayer. At last, on the way from Jerusalem to Damascus, Paul surrendered and fell upon his face, and cried, "Lord, what wilt thou have me do?" He then rose to his feet to do the work of an evangelist. He, along with certain nameless nobodies, went about over the Roman Empire establishing little "colonies of heaven."

These colonies were made up of men and women who did not fear the world's fears. They were men and women who were not gripped by the world's greeds. They were not divided by the chasms that divided others. The pagan world looked on with wistful wonder and exclaimed, "How these Christians love each other!" And because they wanted to love and be loved, they were drawn into these little groups. Thus the Lord added unto them day by day such as were being saved. And as they increased in numbers, they increased in power. Out from them flowed rivers of living water that had a perfectly amazing capacity for withering all that was selfish and unclean, and for making all that was beautiful to grow. The Roman Empire took knowledge and tried to destroy them. But the more they were killed, the more they lived. At last they became so mighty that they displaced the Roman eagle with the cross. Then they began to fear the world's fears, and to be gripped by the world's greeds. Then the sun went down and the night came on, the night of the Dark Ages that lasted almost a thousand years.

Then centuries went by, and England is in the throes of a terrible reaction from Puritanism. And Christianity seems to many a dead and exploded theory. But one night there came out of a little service in Aldersgate Street a man who declared that he had felt his heart strangely warmed. That man mounted his horse the next day and set out on an evangelistic tour that carried him literally through the century. And out of his hot heart there breathed upon England a veritable gulf stream. At the kiss of its warmth the icicles fell from the eaves of the houses, the winter-stripped trees put on their verdant foliage, the flowers bloomed, the birds sang, and the heart stood up in the glad consciousness that God had come. Every reader of history knows today that by far the biggest event of that eventful century was the evangelism of John Wesley and his followers.

III

And now we come to our bewildered and perplexed day. It is a day of cynicism, a day of disillusionment, a day of bitter hunger of heart. Some poet a century from now might sing of large areas of the life of our day:

"On that hard pagan world, disgust and secret loathing fell,
Deep weariness and sated lust made human life a hell."

Multitudes are "between two worlds, the one dead, the other powerless to be born." But our desperate need is at once our challenge and our opportunity. Surely multitudes both within the Church and out of it are realizing as never before that there is none other name under Heaven given among men whereby we must be saved but the name of Jesus.

The call of the hour, therefore, is for the right kind of evangelism. It is only as we evangelize that we shall build up the body of Christ. Doing the work of an evangelist builds up the evangelist himself. There are multitudes even in our churches to whom Jesus Christ is as vague and dim as the shadow of a dream. Is there a roadway to spiritual certainty? I am sure that there is. Jesus is still coming to seek and to save that which is lost. If you and I set out on the same quest, our roads and his are sure to run together sooner or later. We will come face to face with the Christ who is doing what we are undertaking to do. For if any man is willing to do his will, he shall know. We shall also build by capturing from without. It has been my habit through the years to give an opportunity at every service for men and women to make a public confession to Christ. Many times I have called when nobody has responded, but the vast majority of calls have not been in vain.

While seeking the lost we are to realize that our most fruitful work is not with adults, but with childhood and youth. It is still hard for some to believe this.

A fine old gentleman said to me after a service that I had had with the boys and girls, "I do not believe in services of that kind." "Why," I asked? "Because," he said, "ten or twenty years from now some of those boys and girls could not tell you when they were converted." "What of it?" I asked. "Why," he said, with vehemence, "I would not give the pop of my finger for any man's religion who could not tell you the day and the hour in which he was converted." Now if you know when you were converted, thank God for it, but remember this, there may be one sitting beside you who is more beautifully conscious of the Divine Presence than you are, who does not know.

When I was a boy, my father gave me a little colt. He gave me that colt the very day it was born. I began at once to get on good terms with it. I would rub its nose and stroke its ears. Now and then I would give it an apple core (if I could spare it). Then at last I dared to mount that colt and go for a ride. Never once did he throw me, nor kick me, nor paw me. If you had asked that colt three years later, "When were you converted into a work horse?" he would have doubtless answered you in the language of Socrates, "Search me."

But there was another colt about the same age as mine to which nobody paid any particular attention. One day my father said that he was old enough to be converted into a work horse. Therefore we chased him out of a pasture into the lot, and out of the lot into a stable. We bridled and harnessed him and plowed him beside a maturer horse. Then we un-hitched him and let him out to where the ground was soft. We called a colored friend in whom we had a personal interest and asked him if he would be so kind as to mount. And when he mounted, the back of that colt went up like the apex of an isosceles triangle, and the colored brother erased himself. Finally, after he had thrown a few more men, after he had torn up one or two pairs of harness, and kicked the spatter board out of the buggy, a strong man could drive him pro-vided he was tired. If you had asked him three years later when he was converted, he would have said, "I shall never forget it as long as I live. It was a terrible ordeal." But I submit to you that my colt was broken in a far more normal and a far more natural way. All of which leads me to say that the best field of evangel-ism is the home, for the only sure way to have Chris-tians is to raise them.

Finally if we are to do the work of an evangelist, we must be willing to pay the price. Evangelism is costly. There is no twilight sleep process for the bring-ing of new-born souls into the Kingdom. It is only as Zion travaileth that she brings forth sons and daugh-ters. That is the reason that an ease-loving Church like ours shies away from it. We do not like to be bothered. The passionate words of the saints sound to us a bit like a foreign tongue. "And now, behold, I go bound in the spirit unto Jerusalem, not knowing the things that shall befall me there; save that the Holy

Ghost witnesseth in every city saying that bonds and afflictions abide me. But none of these things move me." And here is rugged John Knox crying, "Give me Scotland or I die." We rather say, "Give me a comfortable bit of Scotland, or I will move." Too few of us believe in evangelism enough to be eager to pay the price. But where the price is paid results are sure.

Several years ago I was conducting a revival in a little town where there were seven or eight churches that had just enough interest to quarrel among themselves. The meeting was going badly, and I was desperately discouraged. At last I tried to have a testimony meeting, and the testimonies dwindled into discouraging and critical sermonettes. Just as I was preparing to close the service in despair, a gentleman stood up, that I came to know intimately, and to honor and love with genuine devotion. His presence was not prepossessing. He was rather shabbily dressed. He used bad grammar. But what redeemed him from commonplaceness was a marvelously illuminated face. It looked like it had a sunrise behind it, and you felt yourself almost unconsciously peeking round to see where the light came from. He turned that wonderful face toward me and said, "Brother, I thank God that things are just as they are." I looked at him in wide-eyed amazement. But he went on to explain. "I love to get in a hard place for my Lord. I love to get in a place that is so hard that there is no chance to get into without you get down on both hands and knees and crawl through to God." I saw that he knew a secret which I was too little familiar. After this testimony, we dismissed, and went home.

In the evening service that followed, the tabernacle was crowded to overflowing. There was a mourner's bench that ran entirely across the tabernacle. It was long enough to have accommodated at least a hundred mourners, though one an inch long would have been long enough for what we had been having. I stepped out on this mourner's bench and began my sermon. I had been preaching only two or three minutes when this brother came and kneeled down beside me, and as he prayed I tried to preach. And, account for it how you may, the atmosphere was utterly changed. I saw strong men come from out the dark to kneel at the altar, but before they could get on their knees they rose into newness of life. "And the place was shaken where we were assembled together, and we were all filled with the Holy Spirit." And it is my conviction that the Church will never rediscover the lost secret of its evangelistic power till it learns again the high art of prayer. Let us therefore take to heart the challenging words of our text, "Do the work of an evangelist."

IX

A GOOD MAN'S BLUNDER

(GO-TO-CHURCH SUNDAY)

*"And he did that which was right in the sight
of the Lord, according to all that his father
Uzziah did: howbeit he entered not into the
temple of the Lord. And the people did yet
corruptly."*

II CHRONICLES 27: 2

I

HERE IS AN ANCIENT STORY THAT IS EXCEEDINGLY
modern. The hero of the story is Jotham, onetime king in Jerusalem. He was doubtless a bit in a
class to himself in that distant day. But he would
find himself a part of a great multitude were he living
now. It is evident that the author has a genuine admiration for Jotham. As we read this all-too-brief
biography we are not surprised. He had certain sterling and worthful qualities that demand admiration in
every age.

1. He was a man of fine native gifts. He was a
king by right of birth; but he was far more, he was
king by right of ability. He had qualities of leadership
and of intellect that fitted him for his high office. He

was no crowned nonentity. He was no sceptered incompetent. He had royal gifts to match his royal position.

2. Not only was he a man of ability, but he was also energetic. He was willing to work. I have known men of fine gifts to neutralize their usefulness by a halfhearted exercise of their powers. But this was not the case with Jotham. He believed that he had not come to be ministered unto, but to minister. He refused to be a parasite. He was an earnest and active servant of his people. He was a keen and courageous warrior, a wise and constructive statesman.

3. Not only was he an able and energetic worker, deeply concerned about the material interests of his people; not only did he build fortresses for their protection and cities in which they were to live, but he was concerned for their spiritual welfare. He was wise enough to realize something of the supreme importance of the spiritual. He was also convinced that these spiritual values were sustained and forwarded by the Church. Therefore, he regarded the Church, not as a liability, but as an asset. So regarding it, he neither opposed nor ignored it, but contributed to its support. The author tells us that he had builded one of its gates. He donated what would today be the equivalent of a memorial window or a pipe organ.

4. Then, best of all, he was a man of fine character. His good deeds were but the natural expression of a good life. The author tells us that he ordered his life

before the Lord his God. That is, he was possessed of a sense of God. He lived as ever in his Great Taskmaster's eye. He affirms, further, that, so living, he did that which was right in the sight of the Lord. This does not mean, of course, that Jotham was an absolutely perfect man. It does mean that the main bent of his life was toward goodness. He was an able, honest, and God-fearing man.

II

But having said all these complimentary things, the author has one adverse criticism. He has one fault to find. At least he counts it as a fault. Of course we have to confess that such conduct is not so regarded by vast multitudes in our day. Some look upon it as a positive virtue. They regard it as a mark of intelligence and broad-mindedness. To refer to it, therefore, as a fault would provoke a smile in many circles, if not loud and scornful laughter.

What was wrong with Jotham? It was not that, though outwardly clean, he was corrupt in his private life. It was not that he was a grafter, using his high office for the feathering of his own nest. He was a good man, remember, constantly ordering his life before the Lord his God. He was genuinely religious. Nor was he at fault in that his religion made him narrow-minded and intolerant toward others. He did not contend so earnestly for the faith that he consigned all who differed from him to the bottomless pit.

His one fault was this—"He entered not into the temple of the Lord."

How trifling! How like "much ado about nothing" such criticism sounds to our modern ears! How narrow-minded and silly to condemn this able and zealous servant of the people merely because he does not take time to attend the services of the Church! This seems doubly so when we face the fact that there were doubtless multitudes of people in Jerusalem who never missed a service at the Temple, who would have looked like moral and spiritual dwarfs if they had stood beside this public-spirited and patriotic king. But in spite of all these considerations this old-fashioned author cannot give Jotham his whole-hearted approval. With a bit of a sob in his throat he writes this one criticism: "He entered not into the temple of the Lord."

III

Why, I wonder, did Jotham refuse to attend church?

Had you talked this question over with this excellent king, there are certain reasons, popular enough in our day, that I am sure he would not have given. For instance, he would never have accounted for his absence on the grounds that there were so many hypocrites in the church. He was far too honest to have given such a sham reason. Those who give that reason are never quite sincere. They are always a bit hypocritical themselves. Nor would he have excused himself on the ground that the preacher was always begging for money, or forever talking about hell. He was not so miserly as to feel that being reminded of his obligation to give partook somewhat of the pangs of hell. Then I am quite sure that Jotham would not have told you that he could worship God on the golf course quite as well as in the Temple. Least of all would he have had to confess that he was staying away from church because he was unwilling to be challenged with responsibilities that he did not have the gallantry and consecration to meet. He was far too fine a man to have remained away for any of these reasons.

What, then, I repeat, were his reasons?

1. One reason, I dare say, for Jotham's absence was that he had never formed the habit of church attendance in his boyhood. Those who attend our services today are, as a rule, those who formed a habit in their young and tender years. In saying this, I am not forgetting the man who tells us that the reason he does not go to church is because he was forced to go when he was a boy. I have met this gentleman. He has told me of his strict upbringing, of what a terrible bore Sunday used to be, of how a mere whistle from his lips on that awful day used to cause him to have to memorize whole chapters of the Bible. But when we ask him to quote one of those numberless chapters, the best he can ever do is "Jesus wept." Often he has even forgotten that, notwithstanding the fact that we remember best what we learn in childhood. There are doubtless those with whom certain pious parents made great mistakes. But

having confessed this, I am convinced that for every one man who never attends church today because he was compelled to go as a boy, there are ten thousand who do not attend because they did not form the habit in childhood.

2. The second reason for Jotham's absence was that he felt no especial need of church attendance. He was young and successful. He had not yet barked his shins against life's grim realities. Then, his hands were full to overflowing with big and worth-while tasks. He was busy organizing and leading armies, in building cities and forts, in the shaping of the destiny of a nation. "Doing good," he would have told you frankly, "is my religion. Why should I turn aside from these big enterprises to go to church and hear some preacher who possibly does not possess one-half of my ability?" And surely there are multitudes that are in hearty agreement with him today. Some of them are excellent people. The majority of our writers of fiction would lead us to believe that they are about the only excellent people. All the really worth-while men and women that we meet on their pages are the nonchurchgoers. Those who attend church are usually narrow-minded and selfish, bending all their efforts to escape from a needy world where they are doing nothing, into a heaven where they can do still less.

Of course we who belong to the Church cannot fully agree. While confessing that many excellent people ignore the Church, we dare to affirm that the supreme spiritual giants of the centuries have not done so. Michael Faraday, the great English chemist and physicist, looms large as he reads a learned paper before the leading scientists of London. We are impressed when we hear no less a personage than the Prince of Wales make a motion to give him a vote of thanks. But we are more impressed still when we discover that the great scientist is not present to receive his vote of thanks. He has slipped out to attend a prayer meeting in his own church—a prayer meeting that was so small and insignificant that there were seldom as many as twenty present. Jesus himself was an exceedingly busy man. His hands were full of great deeds. "He went about doing good." But he was not too busy to attend church. "He went up into the synagogue on the Sabbath, as his custom was." The fact, therefore, that Jotham's life was so full that he felt no need of the Church does not prove that no such need existed.

3. The third reason why Jotham refused to attend Church was that he was prejudiced. I am not sure that this young king would have acknowledged this. I am not sure that he was aware of it himself. But he was a bit prejudiced nonetheless. This, I say, in spite of the fact that he was a good man. That was a good man, an Israelite without guile, who asked the question: "Can any good thing come out of Nazareth?" But he had a prejudice in spite of his goodness. Those of you who have read *I Follow the Road* will doubtless acknowledge that its author is an intelligent and cul-

tivated woman. She also has a vital religious experience. But in spite of this, she is still genuinely prejudiced against ministers and churches in general—this notwithstanding the fact that it was a minister of the Church, Stanley Jones, who led her into her transforming experience.

The cause of Jotham's prejudice is not hard to find. His father was a devoutly religious man. He was a man, also, who loved power. One day, swollen with pride, he dared to take upon himself the office of priest. The officiating priest withstood and rebuked him. Uzziah became exceedingly angry. While his face was red with rage, the mark of leprosy became clearly visible upon his forehead. He was compelled to leave the Temple and to spend the remainder of his life in retirement. He never attended church after that. And Jotham never forgot that horrible experience. He knew, of course, that it was not the priest who gave his father the leprosy, nor was it the Church. Still he had nursed a prejudice against the Church and its ministers ever since.

There are many like that today. Sometimes their prejudice is born of sheer ignorance. The Church is a faulty institution, always has been, because it is made up of faulty folks. It is certainly a long way from being above criticism. But it is unfortunate that the criticism that one reads in modern magazines is generally from twenty-five to fifty years behind the times. This is the case because, as a rule, these critics have little or no first-hand knowledge of the matters of which they write. They are blissfully unaware of what the modern Church is standing for and what it is undertaking to do. Therefore, too often their criticism is born of prejudice that is the outgrowth of ignorance.

At other times such prejudice is based upon a more solid foundation. Some have been disappointed in a particular church. They have found its membership and ministry too lacking in passion for individual and social righteousness. Possibly they may have even suffered wrong at the hands of some member or some official of the church. A young woman told me such a story not long ago. She had been greatly wronged, and the villain was a minister. She had a perfect right to regard this particular minister as a scoundrel. But without discrimination, she had come, on his account, to discredit all ministers in all churches. Worse still, she had repudiated religion altogether. This was, of course, at once unfair and unreasonable. But in spite of its unreasonableness she, as Jotham, had allowed herself to become a victim of her own prejudice.

4. But perhaps the supreme reason why this public-spirited king never went to Church was because he did not take time to sit down and think the matter through. Had he done so he would have realized how inconsistent it was for him to undertake to build up the Church with one hand while he was tearing it down with another. He would have realized the foolishness of giving to the Church, while at the same time he

acted toward it in a fashion that, if followed by his fellows, would have resulted in its absolute destruction. Then, too, had he thought, I am sure that this good man would not have judged the services of the Church solely with reference to their helpfulness to himself personally. He would have taken into consideration their helpfulness to others, his weaker brethren. He would have remembered that the only glimpse that some of his people got of God came through the services of the Church, and he would have supported the Church by his presence for their sakes. But failing to think, he failed to attend.

IV

What was the outcome of his blunder?

One would expect to read that he had exact poetic justice meted out to him; that he ceased to be a good man and died a moral and spiritual bankrupt. That has been true of many who have followed his example. But such was not the case with Jotham. He remained a good and upright man to the end of the day. His failure to attend church did not work his own destruction. Neither did it work the destruction of the Church. By his failure to attend, he no doubt weakened the Church. It would have been more effective if he had been there. The Church needs every man, but no single man is essential. Jotham, by neglecting the Church, neither destroyed the Church nor himself.

What then was the outcome?

The author puts it in a single sentence, "The people did yet corruptly." There were many who admired and honored this able king. They were eager to be like him, but they knew little of his secret prayer life. They did not possess his faith. They did not have his stamina. The good they saw in him, they attributed to himself alone. His religion got no credit. Therefore, when they sought to be like him, they joined him only in ignoring the Church. Thus, while he made the harbor, they became shipwrecked. The tragedy of Jotham's life, therefore, was not so much in the positive harm that he did, but rather in the positive good that he failed to do. He did not fight the Church, but he refused to give it his active support and to help lead it in any aggressive battle for righteousness. For this reason, he left many leading mean and corrupt lives that might have been living nobly and unselfishly if he had only been faithful to the Church of his fathers.

Now, the story of Jotham is far more up-to-date in this hour than the day it was written. One cannot but think wistfully of many fine and right-thinking people outside the Church whose ideals are largely our own who could help us so much if they would. But they stand aloof. One cannot but think more wistfully still of the many Jothams inside the Church, men and women who are well-wishers, who contribute of their means, but who seldom or never attend. Thus, they "damn with faint praise, and without sneering teach the rest to sneer." If only those of us who are within the Church, who believe in its ideals and objectives, would give ourselves conscientiously and aggressively to the achieving of those objectives, we could really make the Church the salt of the earth and the light of the world, and civilization would move into a new day. But so long as we give anything less than ourselves, we may count on it that the record for us will be that of Jotham, "The people did yet corruptly."

X

THE LAY PREACHER

(LAYMAN'S DAY)

"Noah, a preacher of righteousness"
II PETER 2: 5

THIS IS NOT A STARTLING TEXT. HOW RASH TO undertake to interest a modern audience by talking about somebody that came out of the ark! Then my rashness seems greater still when we discover that this somebody was a preacher. Preachers are not universally interesting. The very mention of the word leads some folks to stifle a yawn. There are still those who feel that society should be divided into three classes—men, women, and preachers. This, in spite of the fact that whenever a minister becomes more preacher than man, he ought to quit the ministry and take up some other work.

We are indebted to Peter for calling our attention to the fact that Noah was a preacher. We have not been accustomed to think of him in that light. His reputation as a preacher was in large measure destroyed by the flood. We think of him as a shipbuilder. He was an architect, and strange as it may seem to some, he was quite a good one. Mr. E. H. Rigg, of the New York Shipbuilding Corporation, calls attention to the fact that some of the ships that are being built today have practically the same dimensions as those of the ark. He declares that Noah knew something of ship-building, and that naval architects of modern times are not ashamed to acknowledge their indebtedness to him. But, though he built a first-rate ship, and though he proved himself a sailor of first-class ability, his supreme claim upon our attention is that he was a preacher of righteousness.

Now, in saying that Noah was a preacher, the Apostle does not mean, of course, that he was pastor of some antediluvian church. He doubtless never spoke from a pulpit. He preached by what he was and by what he did. And that is always the most important preaching that any of us do. In that fashion, all of us preach, and preach every day. Sometimes we of the pulpit preach some very dry and poor sermons. There are those who do not hesitate to tell us so. But, as has sometimes been pointed out, we often hear some very poor sermons from the pew. That, for instance, was a poor sermon that you preached when you moved into the city and brought your family and furniture; your car and card table; everything, in fact, for which you cared; and left your family altar and church member-ship behind. That was a rather poor sermon that you delivered when you got so busy with your business that you had no time for recreation except on Sunday.

That was a perfectly rotten sermon that you preached when you drank with the crowd, and thus cast your vote on the side both of lawlessness and drunkenness. Indeed the pulpit does some poor preaching, but it is far from holding a monopoly of that sorry work. Sad to say, the pew also does its share.

I

Noah's Equipment. What equipment did Noah have for the work of the ministry? Nothing is said as to his eloquence, nothing as to his educational advantages, nor his personal magnetism. But the record does tell of certain fundamental qualifications that he possessed that are as necessary today as they were in the days before the flood.

1. Noah walked with God. That means that one day Noah met God and became conscious of his presence. How he made this contact, we do not know. God may have dawned upon him like a sunrise. He may have burst upon him with the suddenness of the lightning's flash. But, however the discovery was made, Noah came face to face with God. And, having met God, nothing else seemed so worth-while as to keep in his fellowship. It was then that life for Noah arose out of the drab commonplaceness of mere existence into the bracing heights of friendship with God. He could say even in that far-off day, "He that hath sent me is with me." And surely this is a fundamental need of everyone who is to have an effective ministry.

2. Noah listened to God. "The Lord spake unto Noah," the record tells us. Of course, but Noah was not the only man in that day to whom God spoke. God speaks to every man in every age. It is easy for us to believe that he spoke in that far-off day, because he is speaking in the here and now. Through varied voices, he is speaking to you and to me. He is speaking through the voice of the better man and woman that we know it is possible for us to be. He is speaking through his word, through his providences, through our joys and sorrows, our laughter and our tears.

What, then, is the difference between Noah and the men of his generation? It is not that God loved Noah and did not love his fellows. It is not that God singled out Noah to speak to him, while to all others he was silent. The difference is rather in this—when God was broadcasting, Noah tuned in on him, while his fellows listened only to the voices of the world. It was this tuning in that enabled Noah to preach. He who would speak for God must, first of all, listen to him. The true preacher, in the pulpit or pew, must be able to hear the word from God's lips and warn men from him. Happy is he who can say with Isaiah, "Thou hast given me the tongue of him that is taught, that I might know how to speak a word in season to him that is weary."

3. Noah was perfect. Now that is a rather shocking statement. Frankly, we do not like perfect folks. We do not even believe that they exist. Yet the Bible does

say emphatically that Noah was perfect. What does the author mean by such a declaration? Certainly he does not mean that Noah had reached a height of moral and spiritual maturity that made any further progress at once needless and impossible. Neither does he mean that Noah had reached a height where he was no longer tempted. Those who have become thus perfect have run clean past Jesus, and are looking back at him. He was tempted in all points like as we are. No more is it claimed that Noah had become so good that he was incapable of sin. I fancy that I can guess what some of you are thinking. You are remembering that this perfect man had a shameful fall. Yes, so he did. I am not going to blink the fact, because the Bible does not. When we write the biography of our heroes, we tend to gloss over their failings, but not so with this honest Book. It is not afraid to point out the worst as well as the best.

Here is the story: Noah planted a vineyard. In this vineyard he raised some lovely grapes. Now, he reasoned that those grapes were his own, and that he had a right to do as he pleased with them. He believed in personal liberty. Therefore, he took some of them and made a bit of home brew. Quite a modern man was Noah! Not only did he make home brew, but he drank it. Not only did he drink it, but as often happens, he drank too much. So he got beastly drunk. And strange to say, even in that far-off day, drunkenness does not look good. We cannot read the story without feeling that Noah has done a shameful and sinful thing. Therefore, in saying that Noah was perfect the author does not mean that he was sinless. He means rather that he was whole-hearted in his devotion to God. Scriptural perfection means a unified personality.

Now, Noah had a son named Ham. It is evident that Ham did not believe in the Eighteenth Amendment. Therefore, when he saw this staid and upright lay preacher three sheets in the wind and worse, he was sure that prohibition did not prohibit, and it filled him with glee. It was a story too good to keep, so he broadcast the distressing news all over the community. And what was the outcome? Unless you have some poetry in you, you should not read this story. Ham was cursed for his broadcasting. The curse was that he became black—that is, his skin became the color of his heart. Yet, strange to say, it was not Ham that drank the home brew; Noah, the lay preacher, did that. But the curse was not upon the man who got drunk, it was rather upon him who rejoiced in his downfall. Drunkenness is a sin, but it is not so deadly a sin as that of rejoicing over another's tragic fall. How different was the conduct of Ham's two brothers! They refused even to look upon their father's shame. Instead, they spread the mantle of charity over it. Thus they showed themselves possessed of the spirit of Christ long before Christ was born.

Then, it is interesting to notice the time of Noah's

fall. He did not fall in those stressful years when he was building the ark. He did not fall during the grim days of depression, when the world was submerged. It was when the hard times were over, when he had come upon times of luxury and ease, that he fell. These are hard days for many of us, but luxury is always a sharper test than poverty. There are many who are thinking of God today who had no time for him a few years ago. "Your business has at least kept up," I said to one of our leading undertakers last week. "No," he answered, "you are wrong. The death rate has fallen off decidedly since the depression set in. Folks can't live so fast, nor eat and drink so much." Days of poverty are dangerous, but days of great material prosperity are more dangerous still. But, in spite of his fall, the main tenor of Noah's life was whole-hearted devotion to God. He walked with God, and listened to God, and God used him as his spokesman.

II

His Congregation. What kind of folks were those to whom Noah had to preach? It is striking how like they are to ourselves. Jesus emphasizes the fact that there was no great difference between Noah's congregation and his own. "As it was in the days of Noah, so shall it be in the days of the Son of Man." Look at some of their characteristics.

1. Noah's congregation was made up of materialists. They were worshipers of physical force. "There were

giants in those days," the record says. That is, there were men who were conspicuous for their vast bulk and brutish strength. Their power was of brawn rather than brain, physical rather than spiritual. And what was the attitude of that generation to those men of small souls and big fists? Here is the answer. "These were the men of renown." It was a generation, then, when a good athlete in a university was held in greater honor than the chancellor of that institution. It was a time when a mauler outranked a missionary; when a prize fighter could make as much in twenty minutes as the President of the United States could make in ten years. These were worshipers of the god of force.

2. "The world was full of violence." Worshiping physical force, they made the largest possible use of it. It was, therefore, a time of lawlessness, of rebellion against all constituted authority. They had no sense of God. Having become separated from God, they became separated from each other. "Where there is no vision, the people cast off restraint." There are not a few earnest men in our day who are seeking to build a brotherhood. But some of these have no sufficient foundation. They are seeking to build this brotherhood upon our common kinship to the dirt. It is an impossibility. The only sufficient foundation for the brotherhood of man is the fatherhood of God. When men love God, they love each other. When they refuse to love God, they cast off restraint, and the world becomes full of violence. Were Noah to come back to us

today, he would see many familiar faces. Multitudes of our time have lost their vision. Our world is full of violence. Our very lawlessness calls loudly to America to come back to God.

3. A final characteristic of Noah's congregation was its spiritual blindness. They failed to see that their moral rottenness was opening the way to the coming judgment of God. They had become so utterly blind that they believed they could gather grapes of thorns and figs of thistles. They believed that they could sow rottenness and reap soundness; that they could sow injustice and reap a permanent and well-ordered society. They forgot that sin finds the sinner out individually and nationally. Thus they rushed in utter blindness upon their doom.

III

Noah's Theme. What was the theme of Noah's preaching? Any Sunday school boy feels able to answer this question. "The theme of Noah's preaching," you reply readily, "was the flood." But in so saying you are mistaken. His theme, as we learn from the Apostle Peter, was the old-fashioned, arresting, time-honored theme of righteousness. Of course he had something to say about the flood. But when he spoke of the flood he did not speak of it as something that was inevitable. It was inevitable only if people refused to become righteous, if they failed to repent. He tried to make it plain that the supreme tragedy of sin is, not that

the sinner should cease to live, but that he should cease
to be fit to live.

In preaching righteousness, this old-fashioned minister sought to bring home to the consciences of his
hearers their lack of righteousness. He tried to bring
to them the realization that they had sinned and come
short of the glory of God. This he tried to do by
pointing out the wrongs of which they were guilty.
This he also sought to do by showing them the quiet
strength and courage and beauty of his own life. In
the light of his own spiritual winsomeness, he tried to
bring home to them their ugliness. By every power
at his command he sought to emphasize the grim,
devastating fact of sin, the sin of the individual and
the sin of the group.

Not only did Noah seek to bring home to the hearts
of his hearers the fact that they were not righteous,
but he urged upon them the absolute necessity of
their being so. He insisted that they simply could
not live without it, that to refuse to be right was to
rush upon certain death. And this passionate insist-
ence upon righteousness has been characteristic of the
prophets and spiritual leaders of all the centuries. For
instance, when Paul preached before Felix, he reasoned of righteousness. On another occasion he declared that the Kingdom of God is not eating and
drinking, but righteousness, and peace, and joy in the
Holy Spirit. It is our task to proclaim, with far clearer
vision than that of Noah, the necessity for righteous-

ness. Man must be right with God. He must be right with himself, right with his fellows, right in his business and industrial relations. There must be rightness between race and race, between nation and nation. We must make men see that this is a doomed world unless it becomes a righteous world.

Finally, Noah undertook to show his blind and sinning congregation the way of righteousness. Of course, he lived in the twilight, while we live in the noonday. The trail for him was very dim, while for you and me it ought to be as clear as a broad highway. How may one who is wrong become right? The answer is proclaimed upon almost every page of the Bible. The way of righteousness is the way of repentance. It is the way of turning from sin to God. "Let the wicked forsake his way, and the unrighteous man his thoughts; and let him return unto the Lord, and he will have mercy upon him, and to our God, for he will abundantly pardon." This is the wide-open road, and there is no other. It is Jesus himself who warns, "Except ye repent, ye shall all likewise perish."

IV

His Results. What was the outcome of Noah's preaching? He had a long ministry. It stretched through toilsome and trying years. How many converts did he win? The answer is very disappointing. So far as the big world was concerned, he did not have one. There were those, no doubt, who admired

Noah. They honored him for his courage and his un-
swerving loyalty to his convictions. Some others
laughed at him for a fool, or pitied him as a madman.
Some, perchance, loved him and lent him a hand at his
shipbuilding. But none of these could quite believe
him. So when the flood came, not one entered the ark
with him. His ministry to those outside his home was
in his own generation a flat failure.

But if Noah failed in the winning of his friends and
neighbors, he succeeded with the members of his own
household. That speaks volumes to his credit. If those
who know us best, if those who see us when we have
the toothache and heartache, when we have not slept
well and everything has gone dead wrong, if these believe in us, then the chances are that we are genuine,
however small the impression we make upon the great
world. This preacher of righteousness won his own
children, and in so doing afforded God a new chance
for the bringing in of his Kingdom.

Finally let us remember that the ministry of this
good man did not end with his home-going. When he
came out of the ark, he offered a sacrifice, and the story
says that the Lord "smelled a sweet savor." That
sounds very crude, as if the odor of burning meat were
pleasant to the infinite God. But the better translation,
as another has pointed out, is that "the Lord in-
breathed a savor of rest." Now, Noah means rest,
and what the passage really means is that the fragrance
of Noah's personality was wafted into the very heavens

and brought delight to the heart of God. And that fragrance has been blown upon the breezes of all the centuries. It has crossed all the seas. It comes in through the windows of this church at this hour, and even we are the better for the fragrance of this holy life that was lived so long ago. Therefore, though this preacher of righteousness won few converts in his own day, there is no measuring the laurels he has won as he has continued to preach through the long centuries.

XI

A SEARCHING QUESTION
(CHURCH BUDGET SUNDAY)

"Will a man rob God?"
MALACHI 3: 8

I

THIS IS A STARTLING QUESTION. THE PROPHET Malachi seems to be gripping his listless people by the shoulders in an effort to shake them into wakefulness. He is seeking to make them face the facts about themselves. Therefore, he flings at them this arresting word: "Will a man rob God?" Will he? I know there are those who will rob the government of which they are a part. I know that there are those who will steal from the coffers of the city that elected them to positions of trust. There are brothers that will rob brothers. There are parents that will steal from their own children, and children that will steal from their parents. But will a man rob God? When we rob each other, we feel that there is a chance that our dishonesty may never be detected. But this cannot be the case when we rob him in whose hand our breath is and whose are all our ways. How, then, shall we answer this question?

Our first impulse is to give an emphatic No. "Certainly not," we are ready to answer with horror. No man would be so mad as to rob God. Somewhere I read this story. One night a certain home was burglarized in the city of New York. In one room that had been looted there was a statue of Christ. This statue was found next morning with its face turned to the wall. This man of crime could not carry on even with the sightless eyes of the statue of Christ looking at him. Certainly, then, a man could not rob the all-seeing God himself. But when we face the facts we find that we are wrong. Men will rob God. There were such in the days of the prophet Malachi. "Ye have robbed me," he declares, speaking for God. It was a fearful charge. Naturally those so accused were indignant. "You have flung at us a horrible accusation," they reply. "Prove it. Cite instances. Tell us wherein we have robbed God."

And what answer does the prophet make? Does he retract his harsh accusation? Does he hasten to apologize? Does he confess, in shame, that he has spoken too hastily, or that he was overstating the case in order to arouse their attention and to startle them? No, he has nothing to take back. On the contrary, he reaffirms his charge and cites instances. "You ask me to be specific," he replies. "All right, I will. You have robbed God in tithes and offerings. By withholding your tithes and offerings you have cheated God of his just dues." It is evident, therefore, that it was the conviction of Malachi, that to refuse to tithe is to be guilty of robbing God. This fact is so plain that it is impossible to fail to understand it.

II

How had these people come to be guilty of robbing God? What excuse did they have to plead for refusing to tithe? They could not plead ignorance. They had known from their infancy that the tenth of all their increase belonged to God. They could not plead poverty. Many of them were poor, as many of us are poor today. But I have known very few people whose poverty prevented their tithing. The truth of the matter is, it is far easier to induce those with small incomes to tithe than those whose incomes are large. Somehow as our incomes increase, we fail to be impressed by the increase of the nine-tenths. We are only impressed by the increase of the one-tenth. The tithers of the Church today are as a rule the poor rather than the well-to-do.

No more had these people ceased to tithe because they had flung away from religion altogether. They still attended church. They still gave after a fashion. But their gifts were small and cheap. Why was this the case? Because they had lost all sense of God's love. When he approaches them at the opening of this prophecy with the declaration, "I have loved you," they answer peevishly, "Wherein hast thou loved us?" They could see no tokens of his love. They were blind to his blessings that were new every morning. Therefore, having lost all sense of his love, they had ceased to love in return; and having ceased to love, they had lost all zest for giving. Love delights to give. It is heartbroken when it cannot give. But when love dies, we give as little as possible.

Such was the case here. These no longer asked, "How much can we give," but, "how little." They no longer brought the best of the flock, lambs without blemish. Instead they brought that which was of least value, the torn, the sick, the worthless. By such giving, the prophet tells them plainly, they were not honoring God, but dishonoring him. "Offer such gifts to thy governor," he suggests, with fine scorn and indignation. "Take your sick sheep to the minister of Artaxerxes, and see how he will receive them." In other words, having lost their love, they were offering to God what they would not have dared to offer to man. They had adopted a financial system by which they were robbing both God and themselves. And I am quite sure that this is the case with many of us today. As these of the long ago, we are robbing God in tithes and offerings.

III

But you reply, "The law of the tithe is an old Jewish law. It is in no sense binding upon us who are Christians." There is something to be said for your position. Yet I am convinced that even we who are Christians should so far as possible give a tithe of our incomes as a minimum. Of course this is not the extent of the obligations of many. Some of us should give far more, because we are able to do so. But everybody ought to try to give at least a tenth. This I say for the following reasons:

1. Tithing is scriptural. At least it is emphatically taught in the Old Testament. Here are the solid facts upon which this demand rests:

(1) God is the absolute owner of everything. "All things were made by him, and without him was not anything made that was made." "The earth is the Lord's, and the fulness thereof, the world, and they that dwell therein." Every foot of land is his. "The cattle upon a thousand hills are his." We are his, his by right of creation, and by right of redemption. To that, I think we all agree. One of the first convictions that came to the Spirit-baptized saints after Pentecost was this: that God is the absolute owner of all. "Neither said any of them that aught of the things that he possessed was his own."

(2) Now, since God owns all, we ought to set aside a certain part of our income in acknowledgment of his ownership. That is only reasonable and right. Men have been gripped by this conviction throughout the centuries. Even those who worshiped many gods felt that they ought to dedicate somewhat of their substance to these gods for their gifts to them. We need to make this acknowledgment as an act of obedience and grati-

tude. We need to make it both for our own good and for the good of others. If we fail to do so, we come to believe that we are the owners of our substance rather than the possessors, a conviction that always leads to spiritual impoverishment.

(3) Finally, since God owns all, and since we ought to make some acknowledgment of his ownership, it is God's right to say what proportion of our substance should be set aside for the making of such acknowledgment. This has been pointed out many times before. I am saying it here, not because it is new, but because it is true. It is his to decide how much of our time is to be holy unto the Lord. We believe that the Sabbath has been given by divine revelation. Jesus declares that it was made for man. By this, he means that it fits into human need. It is not an arbitrary law, like driving on the right-hand side of the street instead of on the left. It is right in the nature of things. The man or the group that observes the Sabbath, other things being equal, will make greater progress physically, intellectually, and spiritually than those who do not. I am just as sure of this as I am of my own existence. We believe, also, that the tithe is a law of revelation. It, too, fits into human need. It is not a law that was made by Moses. It was in vogue centuries before Moses was born. It is the one proportion mentioned in the Old Testament, and it is impossible to shut our eyes to the fact that those refusing to tithe were accused of dealing dishonestly with God.

Now, when we come to the New Testament, we find a fuller and clearer teaching regarding our relationship to property. Jesus had more to say about this than he had to say about repentance. He had more to say about it than he had to say about regeneration. He had more to say about it than he had to say about heaven. He had far more to say about it than he had to say about hell. Almost half of his recorded sayings relate directly or indirectly to money. In his teachings he reaffirmed God's ownership of everything. He taught further that man should administer all his possessions as God's steward. But there is no indication that he repealed the law of the tithe. Instead he gave it his sanction. This he did directly and specifically. For instance, in his denunciation of the Pharisees he said, "Ye pay tithe of mint and anise and cummin, and have omitted the weightier matters of the law, judgment, mercy, and faith." Then he adds, "These ought ye to have done, and not to leave the other undone." That is, the sin of the Pharisees was not tithing. They were right in doing that. They were wrong in trying to make tithing a substitute for right living. Of course tithing is no substitute for character, any more than is prayer. But tithing rightly done bears the direct sanction of Jesus.

Jesus further teaches by implication that we ought to give a tithe as a minimum. He declares that to whom much is given of him shall much be required, that the greater our opportunity the greater our responsibility.

Now the Jews of Malachi's day were living in the twilight, while we are living in the blazing noonday. Yet the tithe was required of them, and they were accounted guilty of robbery when they withheld it. Do you suppose less is to be expected of us with our far greater light? I know that it is objected to tithing that we are not under law, but under grace. That is true. Therefore, to make this a reason for giving more than a tenth is altogether valid. But to offer it as an excuse for giving less is to make the grace of God to minister to our stinginess. It is also to go on the assumption that the greater our opportunity the less our obligation. And this we all know is flatly contradictory to the whole spirit and teaching of the New Testament. Therefore, we may affirm that the giving of at least a tithe is taught both in the Old and the New Testament Scriptures.

2. My second reason for believing in tithing is that it seems to be a thoroughly sane and sensible way of financing the work of the Kingdom. Of course we should naturally expect this to be the case, since it is scriptural. But I am not asking you to adopt this plan solely for this reason. I am rather asking you to adopt it because it is a good plan, a plan that must appeal to your common sense. Of course if you have discovered a better, you ought to use it, but if not, suppose you try this one. I think it commends itself for the following reasons:

(1) It is business-like. It does not leave our sup-

port of the interests of the Church to mere caprice. There are some who pay if they are approached by the right individual. There are others who pay if their emotions are stirred. There are others still who pay if they like the pastor. But such paying is too largely a matter of chance. There is entirely too little conscience in it, and no system at all. But the man who tithes is able to make an intelligent pledge to his church. By such pledging he enables his church to operate on a solid business basis, and this no church can do whose membership refuses to pledge. There are many non-tithers who give but do not pledge. Of course they make a pledge to the grocery man, and to the light man, and to the laundry man, to everyone in fact except to their Lord. But if everyone took that course the church could not operate in a business-like way at all. But tithing is a business-like way for the giver, and it enables the church to be business-like.

(2) Tithing appeals to me as sane and sensible because it makes for the kind of giving that the Lord loves, and that is cheerful giving. There are those for whom any sort of appeal is an offense. There are those to whom giving is about as painful as a surgical operation. But this is not the case with those who tithe. If when money comes into your hands you would at once put aside the tenth as the Lord's, never regarding it for a moment as your own, then when an appeal should come, you would not have to have a battle with yourself. The only question would be what part of the Lord's money

you would put into this particular cause. This would change giving from a pain into a pleasure.

(3) Then, tithing commends itself to our good sense because it is adequate. Many of our churches have been greatly handicapped for lack of funds during these years of depression. We have suffered on our mission fields even more than we have suffered at home. But our financial embarrassment has not been the result of our poverty so much as it has been the result of our failure to follow this sane method of giving. If the whole membership of the Church were to begin to tithe, our days of financial embarrassment would be at an end. We should have ample funds for all enterprises of the Church. As a result I am persuaded that the work of God would go forward in a fashion that would make us both to wonder and to rejoice.

Not only would such giving be adequate in amount, but it would also be timely. Many churches compel their pastors to go into debt for living expenses because they fail to pay them an adequate salary. Then, there are those who pay an adequate salary that drive their pastors into debt because they do not pay when due. Then, too, we constantly make it necessary for our mission boards to borrow money on which they have to pay interest because so many wait till the end of the year to pay their church dues. But the conscientious tither not only pays, but pays when due. When is the tithe due? The answer is plain—when it comes into your hand. This is scriptural. The Bible plainly declares, "The first fruits are the Lord's." If you pay after this fashion you will pay easier. You will pay in a way that will help you honor God and the Church.

3. The final reason I give for tithing is that it is a means of grace to him that practices it. This is the plain promise of the prophet. "Prove me now herewith, saith the Lord." That is, call my hand. Put me to the test. And how are we to do this? We are to bring the whole tithe into the storehouse. That is the divine plan. That does not mean to hold on to every penny you possess till somebody comes and corkscrews it out of your hand. There are those who never give except they are driven to it through a financial campaign. This, I am sure, is better than not giving at all. But it is a poor second best. God's method is this: Bring the tithe into the storehouse. And the promise to those who do so is this: "I will open you the windows of heaven, and pour you out a blessing that there shall not be room to receive it."

It is natural that tithing when rightly done should result in spiritual enrichment. It is an act of faith and obedience. Then, too, it brings a sense of God into our daily task. I have often heard good people bewail the fact that they could not be more constantly engaged in work that is distinctly religious. "If I were only a missionary!" they say. Or, "If I were only a minister!" But there is a way for them to make their daily task just as religious as any minister or missionary. If you are a conscientious tither, then God and you are in partnership. Every penny you make is partly his. The consciousness of this fact will more and more enable you to handle the tools of your daily task as religiously as you handle the communion cup on Sunday morning.

Then, it is natural that tithing should be a means of grace, because the hand that is open to give will also be open to receive. And of course the opposite is also true. The hand that is fast closed cannot receive the infinite treasure that God longs to give. I was reading sometime ago of a little boy who was playing with a costly vase. He thrust his hand into this vase and got it fastened there. In his difficulty he went to his father. But repeated efforts on the part of both of them failed to set him free. At last the father decided to break the vase, though he prized it very highly. So he took his hammer in hand. But just before he hit the fatal stroke he said, "Now, son, make one more effort, open your hand wide and pull straight out." But the little chap looked at him in amazement and said, "Why, I can't do that. If I open my hand wide like you say, I will drop my penny!" And by our close-shut hands we do not only rob God, but cheat ourselves, and bring ourselves into bondage at the same time.

That tithing is a means of grace has been proven by experience. The testimonies of those who have thus found spiritual enrichment would fill volumes. This is true of the individual. It is also true of the group. Some years ago I became pastor of a church whose income was rather pitifully small in proportion to its membership. A goodly number began to tithe and the church prospered and grew. At the end of six years, the financial income of that church had increased almost tenfold. Nobody ever had to solicit anybody for a penny or to collect a penny. It was all brought in. Standing room in that church was at a premium, and seldom ever a service passed without one or more making confession of personal faith in Jesus Christ. And we found that the Lord did open the windows of heaven and pour out a blessing that there was not room to receive.

XII

THE CRIME OF BEING YOUNG
(A SERMON TO YOUNG PEOPLE)

"He despised him for his youth"
I SAMUEL 17: 42 (Moffatt)

I

HERE IS A STORY SO GRIPPING AND HUMAN THAT IT will live forever. Israel is being invaded by an old and persistent enemy, the Philistines. When the armies stand facing each other, a champion comes forward from the ranks of the Philistines and proposes to settle the issue by single combat. Such contests, as you know, were quite common in classical and medieval times. This champion was all that could be desired in the way of brute force. He was nine feet in height. He had a coat of mail that weighed one hundred and fifty pounds. He had a spear like a weaver's beam, and a voice like the roar of a lion. At his challenge, the knees of the most heroic in the army of Israel went weak, and no man dared fight him. Each day this champion renewed his challenge, becoming all the while more arrogant and bold and insulting. Each day the

Israelites refused to accept, thus weakening their morale and becoming more cowed and shamed and hopeless.

At last after forty days of humiliation, reinforcements came. How many a tragic day has been saved by the coming of reinforcements! There was a time when the battle of Waterloo seemed lost to the forces of Wellington. Napoleon was so sure that he had won the day that he went so far as to dispatch a runner to Paris to tell that the victory was his. Then, reinforcements came to the Iron Duke and Napoleon's victory was changed into defeat. When the armies of the Allies were hard pressed during the World War, about the sweetest music that they ever heard was that rather crude song, "The Yanks Are Coming!" It brought new hope to a million hearts.

That should have been the case when David came. His arrival was to mean the dawning of a new day. But nobody believed it. Goliath, the champion, looked upon him with utter contempt. This would not have been so bad had his contempt not been shared by the soldiers on both sides of the line. This contempt found its fullest expression in the biting words of David's own elder brother, Eliab. Saul was more friendly, but the best he could do was to look wistfully at the young fellow and shake his head. He was desperately eager for a champion, but he could see no hope here. "Thou art not able," he murmurs sadly, "for thou art but a youth." What was wrong with David? What was his crime? Why did they receive him with such an utter lack of enthusiasm? There seems only one answer: He was guilty of being young.

Now, age and youth have always had a tendency to clash. Here, for instance, is a story that comes out of the book of Ezra. After Jerusalem had been conquered and her people carried away into exile, it was the fondest dream of certain pious and patriotic Jews that they might once again return to Jerusalem and rebuild their ruined city and restore their desecrated temple. After long years of waiting, their dream has been so far realized that a handful of them has returned and restored the walls and in some measure rebuilt the city. And now they have come to that which was the very climax of their hopes. They are laying the foundation of the temple. When this was done there went up a loud shout of sheer joy. But mingled with this shout of joy were the sobbings of some who seemed utterly brokenhearted. Who were doing the shouting? It was the youth. They were looking ahead. They were thinking what a glorious temple theirs was to be, and how sure they were to meet God in it in the days to come. It was the old folks that were sobbing. They were thinking of the temple that they knew when they were young. It was so much bigger and more beautiful than this one, that a glimpse of it through the haze of memory made them burst into tears.

This clash of age with youth is quite vigorously alive today. You young people certainly have us worried. We are wondering just what you are going to do next.

Not a few of us elders feel that you are about the worst generation the world has yet seen. Then there is little doubt that we are worrying you, not greatly, but enough to be annoying. We are making you wonder just how you are going to get it across to us that we have forgotten the score, lost step, and are at least a half century behind the times. How can you let us know, without hurting us too much, that we are just fossils, kindly fossils maybe; at times harsh and stupid fossils, perhaps; but fossils nonetheless.

Now, while this age-old conflict between age and youth is easy to explain, it is hard to correct. It is so difficult to get springtime and autumn to see each other's viewpoint. You who are young have never been old. Therefore it is hard for you to put yourselves in our places. It is hard for you to realize that soon you, with your burdens and wrinkles and graying hair, will seem prosaic to your juniors as we to you. Then we who are older have such a tremendous tendency to forget that we were ever young. Once we knew everything, even as you. Once, too, we were not absolutely perfect, as surprising as that confession may seem. We forget this, and therefore, fail to put ourselves in your places. Thus our attitude too often becomes one of carping criticism rather than one of sympathy. It was so in the case of David in the long ago. When he came forward eager to help, his elders tried to kill his enthusiasm by finding fault.

II

Look at the charges brought against youthful David. They have a decidedly modern flavor about them.

1. David is accused of seeking a big job while he is making a mess of the one he has. "Why are you here?" asks his indignant brother. "With whom have you left those few poor sheep?" What Eliab means is that David simply will not settle down to the faithful performance of his duty. "You do not stick to your job," he tells him, "as I did when I was a boy." What a familiar falsehood that is, and how utterly useless! "You are bent on beginning at the top," he continues. "You want to build a spire without taking time to lay a foundation. You are eager to get into a hogshead when, as a matter of fact, you are rattling around in the shell of a mustard seed. You must start at the bottom and work up, as I did."

Now, this is a serious charge. This is the case because the only sure way to get ready for tomorrow is to be faithful in the use of today. The best road into a bigger job is the making the most possible out of one that is small. Some of our youth forget this. But David did not. He may have had just a few sheep, but he kept them faithfully. When one night a bear came after one of his lambs, the bear did not get the lamb, but David got the bear. The story is the same when a lion had undertaken a raid on his flock. Though his task was small, and though it was performed under no human eye, he did it faithfully and well, even at the cost of risking his life.

2. David is accused of being forward. "I know your forwardness," says this angry elder brother. "I know how cocksure you are, how certain you are that you know everything. You have absolutely no respect for your elders. You have no reverence for anything nor anybody." That, too, sounds a bit familiar. It is what many of us are thinking of modern youth, and not without reason. It was in some measure true of David. It is possibly yet more true of the youth of today. Certainly you who are young have no disposition to flatter your elders by your too high regard for their opinions. You shock·us by your discussions of subjects once taboo. You shock us even more by your frank confession of delinquencies that our generation would never have thought of confessing. Then when we become alarmed, you regard us with about as much seriousness as a young duck disporting itself upon a pond would manifest toward a fussy old hen that was frantic with fear lest her adopted offspring might not be able to swim. Yes, youth is usually a bit forward. But that is not altogether bad. The certainty that you can improve upon your elders is one of the secrets of your strength.

3. Another charge against David is that of self-will. "I know your self-will," says this indignant brother. "You are bent on having your own way. You are determined to live your own life, to do absolutely as you

please." This is a charge that is especially up-to-date. We seem to be in the midst of a veritable orgy of doing as we please. We are at present about the most lawless nation on the earth. Our biggest single business is crime. The majority of those engaged in the crime business are young. The average age of our present-day criminal is only nineteen years. Self-will is certainly, therefore, one of the besetting sins of the youth of today.

But in this our young people are far more sinned against than sinning. The tragic breakdown did not begin with them, but further back. Many of the safeguards that we older folks knew in our youth have become greatly weakened, or have been thrown into the discard. For instance, our generation has witnessed a weakening of the restraints born of religion. "Where there is no vision, the people cast off restraint." Vast numbers of us elders have lost all sense of God, and have, therefore, cast off restraint. This has told upon our home life. Many of our youth are but shattered fragments of broken homes. Others come from homes where there is no serious effort at right training, either by precept or example. Where self-will is the law of life for so many fathers and mothers it is not surprising that it has put its defiling touch upon some of our youth.

4. The final charge against David is that he is not serious. He is a mere thrill hunter. He cares for nothing but a good time. For instance, he has come to the front just to see the battle. He cares nothing for the

outcome. It matters not to him whether Israel wins or loses, rises to honor, or sinks into shame. All he is concerned about is the thrill of seeing the battle. He is forever seeking something that will pack a punch, that will give him a kick. So age has been prone to think of youth through the centuries. There are many today who are ready to bewail the fact that our young people are so dreadfully wanting in seriousness, that they are so thoroughly flippant. It is a serious charge, and one that is far older than the story of this youthful shepherd lad.

III

But what is the truth about David, as we learn it, not from his critics, but from his own conduct?

1. He is tremendously in earnest. True, he is quite young. The roses of springtime bloom upon his cheeks and the light of morning sparkles in his eye. Yet he is not flippant. Saul himself is hardly more deeply concerned for the destinies of Israel than he. And somewhat of this deep seriousness we dare claim for the youth of today. We have all passed, during recent years, through a bit of a fiery furnace. Nor have any of us come out altogether without the smell of fire upon our garments. Youth bears its wounds and scars even as you and I. But whatever faults we may charge against them, flippancy is not one of them. Not for long, I dare say, has there been a generation of youth more genuinely serious than the one with which we are privileged to work. This is in itself greatly hopeful.

154

2. Then David has a capacity for a fine moral indignation. When he hears the insulting challenge of this giant of brute force, he expects to see the hand of every soldier of Israel leap to the sword. He expects to see every man on tiptoe of eagerness for battle. But when he realizes that the only response that they dare to make the swaggering bully is a tame and spineless submission, his expectancy gives way to shame, and his shame to hot anger. "Who is this uncircumcised Philistine," he asks with glowing cheeks and flashing eyes, "that he should defy the armies of the living God?" We like these brave and burning words, all of us. We are glad to see David refuse to worship the god of things as they are. We rejoice that he will not allow bullying wrongs to go unchallenged today just because they went unchallenged yesterday.

Now, this capacity to blaze against wrong has been a characteristic of youth at its best through the centuries. It is one of the most heartening facts of our day. Social injustice, race prejudice, the hell and madness of war are being challenged and fought today as never before. This is pre-eminently a youth movement. By this I do not mean that all who are engaged in it are young in years. But real youth is not a mere matter of the almanac, it is a matter of the heart. As long as we can rise against wrong in hot indignation we have youth, whatever the calendar may say. But when we come tamely to submit, that means that we are old, however few our birthdays.

"The lamp of youth will be clean burnt out,
But we will subsist on the smell of it.
Whatever we do, we will fold our hands,
And suck our gums, and think well of it.
Yes, we shall be perfectly pleased with ourselves
And that is the perfectest hell of it."

3. Finally, David is possessed of that high virtue that is universally admired. He has courage. It is fine to be in earnest about the things that count. It is fine to be able to burn with a clean indignation against wrong. But even all this is not enough. We must have the grit to do something about it. David might have given vent to his indignation by merely criticizing his elders as they had criticized him. He might have squandered his energies in boasting what he would do in their place, or what he was going to do when he was older and better prepared. But he does not wait for some easy tomorrow when the odds against him might not be so great. With a fine madness that stirs our hearts, he offers to do battle then and there. Then and there he takes upon himself the weighty task of doing the impossible. That is the call to the youth of today. To answer it requires courage of the highest order.

How has David come by such courage? It was not born of his consciousness of superior strength. No more was it the result of his belief in the superiority of his equipment. He knows that in these he is no match for Goliath. His courage was born of his faith in God. He believes that the supreme forces are those that are spiritual. "Thou comest to me with a sword and spear and shield, but I am come to thee in the name of the Lord of hosts, the God of the armies of Israel whom thou hast defied." Here is the secret of courage at its highest and best. "I have set the Lord always before me. Because he is at my right hand I shall not be moved." In the courage born of faith, this youth went forth to battle and to victory.

And now the scene shifts from that far-off time to our desperate and difficult days. Colossal wrongs still stalk abroad, and gigantic evils loll about us unafraid. In our need we appeal to you who are young. It is up to you to help bring in a better day. To this end you were born, and for this cause you came into the world. Of course, you may refuse to heed the call. You may take a coward's way and bewail the fact that the times are out of joint and that you were ever born to set them right. But you may also take the way of faith and courage and throw yourselves whole-heartedly into the fight. If you do this, as I believe you will, your very difficulties will become advantages. You will be enabled to sing with joy as you zestfully press the battle:

> "Blest is it in this dawn to be alive;
> But to be young, is very heaven."

XIII
WHEN GOD FORGETS
(COMMUNION SUNDAY)

"I will forgive their iniquity, and I will re-
member their sin no more."
JEREMIAH 31: 34

I

THE THOUGHT OF FORGETFULNESS ON THE PART OF God is at first a bit jarring. We are not accustomed to associate forgetfulness with him. To speak of his forgetting seems almost to smack of irreverence. We think of forgetfulness as peculiar to ourselves. We regard it, not as a divine, but as a purely human characteristic. Folks do forget, we are keenly conscious of this fact. Forgetfulness is one of our chief infirmities. Of course there is a strictly scientific sense in which we never forget anything. But for all practical purposes it is safe to say that there is nothing that we do not forget.

1. For instance, we forget each other's names. We forget each other's faces. We meet folks again and again that we ought to know, that we do know in a sense, but for the life of us we cannot recall their names.

This has caused many an embarrassment. Sometimes we can get by without our friends knowing that we have forgotten. Sometimes we spring that threadbare substitute, "Your face is familiar." But again and again, in spite of all our efforts to conceal the fact, we find ourselves humiliatingly forgetful of both the names and the faces of people that we really ought to know.

2. We forget our promises. We forget the pledges that we make one to another. For instance, one day you stood beside a woman who loved you. You promised her that you would live with her according to God's holy ordinance; that you would love, honor, comfort, and keep her in sickness and in health, so long as you both should live. You solemnly declared that there should be no divorcement save that written in terms of green grass upon one of your graves. But you have not always been loving, you have not always been loyal. You have forgotten your marriage vows. We often even forget the vows that we make to God. Some of us have forgotten solemn promises that we made to him in times of trouble, or when we stood before the altar the day we became members of his church. We tend to forget our most sacred promises.

3. We sometimes even forget those we love. A writer tells this story. At a certain railroad station he witnessed the unloading of a rather unusual bit of baggage from the baggage car. It was a boy, very pale and frail and weak. The little fellow had lost one of his

legs. When he was taken from the train, he looked wistfully about him as if searching for some familiar face. Evidently he was expecting somebody that did not come. The trainmen next unloaded two little crutches, and, having placed these under the lad's arms, they stood him against the wall. Then the train moved out from the station, and the last the writer saw of the little fellow he was standing there alone. Nobody had come to meet him.

Do you suppose those who loved him had forgotten? If so, it was a cruel lapse of memory. We feel sure, all of us, that we could never forget after this fashion. Yet there are those who are guilty of equally cruel forgetfulness every day. Your mother has looked eagerly day after day for a letter from you. But it has not come. Your wife's heart is aching for a bit of appreciation. Your husband is hungering for something of the tender thoughtfulness of the old days. But these have been disappointed. Of course we have not meant to be cruel, but we have been just the same.

> "And yet it was never in my heart
> To play so ill a part.
> But evil is wrought for want of thought
> As well as for want of heart."

4. Not only do we forget each other, but we forget God. We forget him in whose hands our breath is and whose are all our ways. We forget the Christ of the manger and of the Cross. He knows how prone we

are to forget. That is the reason he gave us the beautiful service that we this day celebrate. He wants us to remember. "This do in remembrance of me." He knows how easy it is for us to forget him. He knows how prone we are to let slip out of our minds that humbling and exalting fact that we were bondsmen and that the Lord our God delivered us. There is absolutely nothing that we do not tend to forget.

But does God also forget? Are there certain things that slip out of his memory? The thought at first horrifies us. It has a tendency to chill our blood. There seems to be perpetual night in such a thought. Does God forget? We read in his Book that he does. But his forgetfulness is of such a nature that it is the mother of hope and not of despair. The sweetest story I could possibly tell you is this: that God sometimes forgets. That is a truth that is as fragrant as the south wind blowing over beds of violets. It is as caressing as the tender hands of a mother. It is as musical as an angel choir. This is the case, not because forgetfulness is good in itself, but because of the nature of that forgetfulness. It is true, not simply because God sometimes forgets, but because of what he forgets.

II

What does God forget? When we say that he is forgetful, we do not mean that he forgets everything, as we do. God never forgets his universe. He has a million solar systems to look after. His stars are as numberless as the sands, but he never forgets one of them. He never forgets even such a small world as this on which we live. It is daylight now and the sun is in the sky. But I am not in the least afraid that God will get so busy that he will forget to put the sun to bed to-night. I am not in the least afraid that the sun will stand just where it is till our continent becomes a parched desert. I am not afraid that there will never be another restful night with its life-giving dews. Nor am I afraid, when the sun is set, that he will forget to bring it to a resurrection. He will remember to crimson the skies with dawn. He will remember to kiss the hilltops with daylight. We are sure, even in the night, that the morning shall come "singing o'er the sea."

God never forgets a single child of his. He tells us that a nursing mother may forget her child, but that he will never forget. He remembers to clothe the lily. He remembers to coffin the sparrow. He assures us, therefore, that he will certainly remember us who are of more value than many sparrows. He is thinking of you at this moment. He is remembering you this holy Sabbath Day. You may be forgetting him. You may be thinking of your business or of your pleasure, or of your heartache, or of your sin. But be assured of this: he is thinking of you. Your friends may have forgotten you, but he has not. He knows where you sit. He knows where you live. He has not lost your street number. He has not lost you in the midst of the rushing crowd.

We need to remind ourselves of this wonderful truth. We know, of course, that we do not count for very much with many people. If you were lying in your coffin today, it would make but very little difference except with an exceeding few. The big old world would move on just the same. It would sleep and wake, laugh and sob, just as if you had never lived or had never died. In the eyes of almost the whole world, you do not count for a thing. But there is One with whom you do count. You count with God.

You recall the story of the drummer boy who, while crossing the Alps in the army of Napoleon, lost his footing and slipped into a chasm. Falling upon the soft cushion of the snow, he was not seriously hurt. But the cliffs so completely shut him in that he knew there was no hope of escape in his own strength. Therefore he began to beat frantically upon his drum in order to attract the attention of his comrades. They heard and were eager to help. But they dared not do so without orders from their commander. Such orders were never given. When the lad saw he was to be left to die, he began beating his own death march. So pathetic was the scene that rough soldiers, hardened by the cruelties and brutalities of war, could not keep from sobbing like little children. But Napoleon was not moved. He was too busy conquering the world to remember an insignificant boy who had been clumsy enough to lose his footing.

But is our Lord like that? Thank God, he is not.

He does not forget the man who has lost his footing. He has time for him who has lost out, who is at the rear of the procession. "A bruised reed shall he not break, and a smoking flax shall he not quench." Our Lord has a place in his heart for the wounded. He remembers the broken in body, the broken in will, and the broken in heart. He is thinking of the bruised people this morning. He is thinking of all of us.

He remembers the very best of our past and present. He remembers every kind and tender word we ever spoke. He remembers every genuine prayer we have ever prayed. He remembers every unselfish gift we have ever given. He remembers every visit we have paid to the sick and to the imprisoned for love's sake and for his sake. He remembers every penitential tear we ever shed.

"I cannot believe it," you are ready to say. Then I ask you, "Did you ever love?" Have you no trinkets about your home that you keep not because of their value, but because of their connection with somebody that has a grip on your heart? What is the value of that old faded flower that you have pressed away between the leaves of a book? No value, except someone that loved you gave it to you years ago. No value, except that you plucked it from the grave of the little baby that slipped out of your arms into the arms of Jesus. Those who love keep things that are of no great value save for their association with the ones that are loved. And Christ has a heart like that. Only it is in-

164

finite in its tenderness. He never forgets a kindness either to himself or to another.

A robber took the part of Jesus one day. You remember the story. Jesus was dying on the Cross. The people were reviling him. Even one of the robbers that was hanging at his side was joining the crowd in its ugly insults. But the other robber took his part. He said to his companion in crime, "Dost not thou fear God, seeing thou art in the same condemnation? And we indeed justly; for we receive the due reward of our deeds; but this man hath done nothing amiss." Then this dying man said to the dying Christ, "Remember me when thou comest in thy kingdom." And what said Jesus? "Today shalt thou be with me in Paradise." And he was not so busy conquering death, hell, and the grave that he forgot this robber. When he stepped into Paradise that day he had a crucified robber by the hand.

If God then remembers the last and the lowest and the least of us, if he remembers every fine thing about us, what does he forget? He forgets only one thing. Hug this fact to your heart and your hope will have a resurrection. Lay hold of this truth and it will sow your soul with flowers. Believe this message and it will serenade your life with celestial music. There is only one thing in all the universe that God forgets, and that is the thing above all else that we should desire him to forget. It is our sin. And this brings me to the text, "Their sin will I remember no more."

III

When is God able to forget our sin? Certainly he does not forget all sin. There is a dark record standing against many of us even now. But what I am here to tell you is that it need not stand a moment longer. Christ is ready to blot it out. He is ready to forget it. On what conditions will he forget? There is only one thing necessary. You must repent. That is, you must turn from your sin to Jesus Christ. You must come to him who "was wounded for our transgressions and bruised for our iniquities." If you do this, he will forgive your sins and remember them no more forever.

Here is a mother with a son who is now a mature man. There was a time when that son was thoughtless and foolish, wild and wicked. There are some gray hairs upon this mother's head that would not have been there but for the heartache that he has caused. There are wrinkles upon her brow that his folly and sin have made. But a few years ago he repented and came to Christ for his cleansing. Since then he has been straight and strong and clean. Today I sit down by the mother of that boy and say, "Was not John a wild rake years ago?" And she looks at me in pained surprise. "Why, no," she answers, "John was always a good boy." In her love she has forgotten. And Christ's heart is like a mother's heart, only infinitely more tender.

Our Lord, then, is ready and eager to forget our sin. What a wonderful gospel! And this he does, not because he shuts his eyes to the facts. His forgetfulness does not mean that he ignores. He forgets because he washes away our stains and heals our ugly wounds. If we are now trusting him, he has forgotten that we ever sinned. If we are now willing to trust him, he stands ready to forgive and to forget. For forgiveness on God's part means far more than the remission of a penalty. It means that he takes us back into his fellowship and confidence and trusts us as if we had never failed him. Even to the most hopeless of us he says, "Go and sin no more." May this be our faith as we gather about this communion table to take the symbols of his broken body and shed blood. And may we make our very own this gracious promise, "I will forgive their iniquity, and I will remember their sin no more."

XIV
THE OFFICIAL BOARD

(INSTALLATION DAY)

"Wherefore, brethren, look ye out among you seven men of honest report, full of the Holy Spirit and wisdom, whom we may appoint over this business. But we will give ourselves continually to prayer, and to the ministry of the word."

ACTS 6: 3, 4

I

OUR TEXT MARKS A FORWARD STEP IN THE ORganization of the early Church. Through the revival that began at Pentecost, thousands of recruits had been brought into the fold. "There were added unto them day by day such as were being saved." Among these new converts were people who, before their conversion, had been far apart. For instance, there were Palestinian Jews and those that were foreign-born. These had had little use for each other. In fact they had heartily hated each other. But their antipathies were now all but forgotten. Having been baptized into one Spirit they were in process of being builded into a brotherhood.

But a situation developed that threatened to destroy this good work. It came about in this wise. Among those accepting this new faith were some who were doubtless disinherited as soon as the news of their rash conduct reached their loved ones. These being cut off from all financial support were soon faced by dire need. It was to meet this need that men like Barnabas came forward and sold all their possessions and put the proceeds at the disposal of their impoverished fellows. The money thus given was administered by the Apostles. But they somehow failed to give satisfaction to all concerned. Being of Palestine themselves, they were quite naturally accused of showing partiality to the Jews of the homeland. This accusation may have been the result of prejudice. But it is more likely that there was some truth in it. You see, these apostles were not expert business men. Besides, they were already heavily loaded with other duties. But whether the charge was just or unjust, disaster was threatening. The Church was in grave danger of being divided.

"There arose a murmuring," Luke tells us. That is quite a familiar sound in this world. It is heard in all our organizations at times, even in the Church. There were those who began to find fault. They began to criticize. They began to say, "I know that Simon Peter is a great and courageous man, but —" "I know that John, the beloved Apostle, used to lean upon the bosom of his Lord, but —." And so the members of the brotherhood began to look askance at each other.

The home-born Jews were threatening to separate into one group, and the foreign-born into another. It is so easy for faulty folks like us to fail in the high art of living together. It is so easy for us to forget that the supreme purpose of Jesus in the world is to build a brotherhood. It is especially arresting and disappointing to find these saints with the shouts of Pentecost still ringing in their ears, suspecting and criticizing each other, and threatening to resurrect old hates that had divided them in their unregenerate days.

But since this really did happen, I am glad that Luke wrote it into his story. It saves us from that almost irresistible tendency to idealize the past, to look backward to find the golden age of the Church instead of forward. How much false sentiment has been wasted in bewailing the passing of "the Good Old Days!" Now, the Good Old Days had something of good in them. But a fair examination of the facts regarding any day of the past is likely to prove disappointing to one who is seeking for perfection. Even the church of that distant day, athrill with the life-giving experience of Pentecost, was not a perfect church. This was the case for the very simple reason that it was made up of imperfect men and women. But, in spite of their imperfections, these showed the genuineness of their Christianity by meeting the situation and settling their difficulties in the spirit of Christ. By mutual consent they chose an official board to which they gave the task of administering the business affairs of the Church.

Thus they not only avoided division, but prepared the way for a new and better day.

II

What was the advantage of this forward movement? Wherein was it good sense, aside from meeting a pressing emergency? Its value, of course, was not in the fact that it enabled the apostles to enjoy a prolonged vacation. When Simon Peter suggested the choosing of this official board, he was not asking for an easier time for himself and his fellow-apostles. "We will give ourselves," he declares, "continually to prayer and to the ministry of the word." They were still to give themselves, and to do so constantly. They were to be just as busy as they had been before. Nor were these seven helpers chosen because the work that they were to do was considered beneath the dignity of the apostles. They were not chosen as men of a lower rank to do a lesser work than that of preaching. There is no thought of rank or dignity here. Nor is there any such thought anywhere else in the New Testament. Princes in the Church, in the sense of those exercising ecclesiastical lordship over their fellows, is foreign to the whole spirit of Christianity. Nothing that we do in the name of Christ can ever be small. The violet is as much a part of God's plan as is the giant redwood tree; and the smallest rivulet, as the Mississippi.

1. The first advantage of choosing this board was this: It set the apostles free to do the particular work

to which God in his providence had called them. They had been called to be ministers of the word. Therefore, they were to give themselves completely to that high task. Before this new departure they had been in danger of taking too much upon themselves. They had been threatened with the tragedy of sowing themselves broadcast. They were now able to say, "This one thing I do." They were now set free to carry out the wise advice that Paul gave to his son Timothy. You remember how in writing to him of the work of the ministry he presses home this most sane admonition, "Give thyself wholly to it."

Now, the danger that threatened these ministers in the long ago has dogged the steps of the preacher all through the centuries. It was never more threatening than it is today. The machinery of the church has grown more complicated with the passing of the years. How easy it is for the modern minister to become cumbered with much serving! How easy it is for him to squander all his energies chasing from one engagement to another, and thus allowing himself to become a man of all work! How easy for him to find his own spiritual impoverishment and that of his church by taking too much upon himself! Let every minister of the word make his own the high resolve of these apostles of the long ago, "We will give ourselves continually to prayer, and to the ministry of the word."

We believe in a definitely called ministry. We believe that every preacher ought to be able to say humbly with his Master, "The Spirit of the Lord is upon me, because he hath anointed me to preach." We believe that he ought to be able to begin every message with "Thus sayeth the Lord." We believe that it is his high privilege and solemn obligation to be able with Ezekiel to hear the word at his mouth, and to warn men from him. But in order to do this, the preacher must be a listener as well as a spokesman. He must resolve with the psalmist to incline his ear and to hear what the Lord will speak.

Now, such listening requires time. We need time to hear God's voice through his own Word. We need time to hear as he speaks through his prophets, ancient and modern. We need time to hear as he speaks in the secret place of prayer. It is those who take time to listen whose word is with power. What a preacher was Isaiah! How did he learn that heavenly art? To what seminary did he go? He went to the one where God is teacher. He was a good listener. "Thou hast given me the tongue of him that is taught that I might know how to speak a word in season to him that is weary." Here is a man with a word for weary folks. And what a large congregation there is of them! He knew what to say to those who were wearied by a burden of sin, who were wearied by too much weeping, by too heavy loads of care. He knew how to change despair into hope, and sobs into songs. So can every minister who will give himself continually to prayer and to the ministry of the word.

173

2. Then, the choice of these men was wise because their help was sorely needed. God has a task for every man. Every man ought to have a share in the bringing in of the Kingdom. The world can never be won through the ministry of the pulpit alone. It was the lay evangelist rather than the preacher that set that ancient world on fire. The layman is no less important today. If we are to keep a growing congregation in First Church, it must not and cannot be left solely to your minister. If men and women are to be won to Christ and built up in Christ by this church, you of the pew have a part to play that is just as vital and important as that of your pastor.

Our tendency to forget this constitutes, in my opinion, one of the chief weaknesses of our denomination. We are prone to place too much of the responsibility for the ongoing of the church upon the shoulders of the minister. If our sister church across the street were to be left without a pastor for a year, it would make no vast difference. The laymen would carry on. They have been trained that way. But if this church were to be left without a pastor for a year, there would be danger of utter disaster. This is the case because your training tends to make you feel that your church belongs to your pastor rather than to yourselves. But please bear in mind that this church is not mine, but yours. You were here before I came. You will likely be here when I am gone. It is, therefore, upon your shoulders that the main responsibility of this church rests. Without you, my hands are tied. Without you, my best efforts will prove little short of futile. But with your loyal and prayerful co-operation, even faltering efforts will result in victory.

III

Look next at the high moral and spiritual standard set for those whose duty it was to look after the business affairs of this church; for those who, as Peter puts it, were to serve tables. Their task seems trivial, even little short of menial. Yet you will notice that those chosen for this work were to live on a plane not one whit lower than that occupied by the apostles themselves. The standard of Christian living for the minister is high, but it is no higher than that for the layman. What was expected of these members of the board?

1. They were to be men of good report. That is, they were to be men about whom good things were reported. They were to be men of good reputation. What a shame to the church when a Sunday school teacher or an official member, or any member for that matter, has to be pointed to with contempt. "Let no man despise thee," Paul wrote to a young Christian of the long ago. And so he writes to you and me. See to it that you do not bring yourself and your church into reproach by the shoddy and ragged and indifferent life that you live. I have known those in official positions in the church to live such ugly lives that, if I had not known

the church itself at first-hand, they would have turned me away from the whole organization in utter disgust.

But, thank God, there is another side to the picture! I have known others so fine and clean and wholesome, so courageous and unselfish, that they commended their church to every thoughtful observer. I have known laymen so beautiful in their lives that if I had not known their church at first-hand, I should have gone immediately to become acquainted with it, saying in my heart, "If that church produces such solid and sterling character as this, I want to know it. Not only so, but I want to become a part of it." Remember that the honor of the church rests upon your shoulders. You are, therefore, to be men of good report.

2. These officials were men full of the Holy Spirit. Now, that does not mean that they were exceptional, abnormal Christians. It means rather that they were beautifully normal. For the Christian that is not spiritual is not in any real sense a Christian at all. "If any man have not the Spirit of Christ," says Paul, "he is none of his." These men were spiritual men, and that is ever the supreme need both for pulpit and pew. God cannot work at his best except through spiritual men and women. Organize dry bones how we may, we have nothing but a skeleton. It takes the Spirit of God to bring life.

3. These men were full of wisdom. That does not mean that they were all university graduates. It does not mean that they were men of peculiarly great intel-

lectual gifts. It rather means that they were men of good, sanctified common sense. It means that they had the type of wisdom that is the very fruit and flower of genuine spirituality. "God has not given us the spirit of fearfulness, but of power and of love and of a sound mind." Few things are better than sanctified common sense, for as another has said, "Common sense is that sense without which all other sense is nonsense."

IV

Why were the requirements of these men whose duty it was to administer the business affairs of this semi-pauper Church so high? Surely it looks as if men of lesser qualifications could have adequately discharged a task that seems so small! But such is not the case. The requirements were thus high, because nothing we do in the Church is an end in itself. If the tasks to which we put our hands were ends in themselves, then, of course, spirituality would not be a necessity.

If, for instance, preaching were an end in itself, anybody could preach who could use the enticing words of man's wisdom. Anybody could preach who possessed oratorical skill. A friend was telling me recently of witnessing the performance of an expert dagger thrower. He stood a woman against a white background and drew her exact profile by throwing daggers in such a fashion that each one seemed to come within the smallest fraction of an inch of her person. Yet he never once drew a drop of blood. He had great skill, but his was the skill of missing rather than of hitting. And I have known preachers like that. They were skilled speakers, but they never drew blood. There were no slain of the Lord ever left on the field after the sermon. Their word was not with power. Preaching is not an end in itself. It is to help forward the Kingdom of God. Therefore, something more is needed than skill in speaking.

The same is true of the teacher in the Sunday school. If the whole task of the teacher were the building up of his class and the imparting of certain scriptural facts, then anybody could teach who had the gift of organization and of teaching. But the Sunday school is the training ground for the Church. Its one purpose is the winning of men and women, boys and girls, to Christ, and of building them up in Christ. Therefore, for this task we need men of honest report, full of the Holy Spirit, and of wisdom.

And just as preaching and teaching are not ends in themselves, no more is the administering of the business affairs of the Church. If such had been the case, then Stephen might have been a pagan, and Philip a Pharisee. But these men are to give the common bread of the church in such a fashion as to make it the very Bread of Life to those who receive it. And this they did. It was these laymen and men of their kind who brought about the rapid spread of the Gospel of Christ. And it is to that same source we must look for the major help for our conquest today.

V

What effect did this first church of Jerusalem with its devoted ministry and its spirit-filled official board have upon the city and upon the world?

1. "The word of the Lord increased in Jerusalem greatly." That sounds as if presses were set to work at once printing new copies of the Bible. But that is not the meaning. The only word that was being printed was in terms of lives remade. The word of the Lord is, as you know, a revelation of God. And what Luke is saying is that upon the streets of Jerusalem appeared men and women who by the radiance and beauty of their lives were revelations of God to men.

2. The further result of the impact of this church upon the city was persecution. That is only natural, for this was a church that made sin afraid. It was a church that made selfishness, meanness, and every form of wrongdoing to tremble in its presence. But this persecution, instead of putting out the fire, only spread it. Instead of making for defeat, it made for a larger victory. "So mightily grew the world of the Lord and prevailed." And like blessed results will surely follow in our day if we meet the conditions. If we who are pastors give ourselves continually to prayer, and to the ministry of the word; if you of the official board dare to be men of good report, full of the Holy Spirit and wisdom, we shall have here a church that will scorn difficulties and laugh at impossibilities. God grant that it may be so!

XV
THAT MAGNIFICENT MINORITY
(THANKSGIVING DAY)

"And one of them, when he saw that he was healed, turned back, and with a loud voice glorified God, and fell down on his face at his feet, giving him thanks: and he was a Samaritan."

LUKE 17: 15, 16

HERE IS A MAN WHOSE ACQUAINTANCE WE SHALL do well to make. True, he is a Samaritan, a creature of a mongrel race. But in spite of that fact he is tremendously worth knowing. I am sorry to tell you that I cannot call his name. He forgot to leave us his autograph. He belongs to that vast company of anonymous helpers who live their beautiful lives and do their worthful deeds without ever taking time to tell us who they are. But, though we do not know his name, we still know enough about him to make us admire him, and even love him. His fine face looks upon us across the far spaces of the years with gripping winsomeness. His personality, after all these centuries, is as gracious and fragrant as the perfume of flowers.

But when we first meet him there is nothing to distinguish him from his fellows. He is a part of a group of ten wretched men that seem to be serving as a kind of reception committee to welcome Jesus to a certain village. But in reality these are not a reception committee at all. They are not brothers in a high and holy service. The bond that binds them together is rather that of a common tragedy. They stagger under the weight of a common woe. So far as we can see, there is nothing to distinguish the heroic one from the commonplace nine. They present one monotonous ugliness.

I

Look in how many respects they are alike.

1. They are all lepers. They all suffer from the same dread disease. They are all facing the same ghastly death. They are all being buried piecemeal by the same horrible gravedigger. They are lepers, and therefore, outcasts, shut out from the consolations of church, and friends, and home. They are abandoned bits of human wreckage, fit only to be flung prematurely into empty tombs. And the one, to all appearances, is just as hopeless as the other.

2. They are alike in their desperate determination to live. Though they seem hopelessly doomed, they refuse to give up. They will not meet death halfway. Faced by grim tragedy, they will not take it lying down. They gamely refuse to die till something actually kills them. I like that. I believe God loves a

brave fighter. These men are full of battle because of their desperate determination to live.

3. They are all possessed of faith in Jesus. This is evidenced by what they do.

(1) When they hear that Jesus is coming their way, they all go out to meet him. Strange rumors have been blowing about the country with regard to This Man. Some were saying that he cared for folks as none other ever cared, that even outcasts were not cast beyond his interest. There were those who were daring to assert that he had even touched lepers into purity. These wild and unbelievable rumors have come to these ten lepers. Of course they find it hard to believe them. But in spite of doubts, they do believe—the whole ten of them. They believe so firmly that they go in a body in search of this amazing Physician who has made them to hope.

(2) Their faith is also indicated by the fact that they not only go in a body to meet Jesus, but, by the further fact, that when they come as close to him as they dare, they appeal to him for help. They are men of prayer, every one of them. They know how to ask in such a fashion as to win through to victory. Then their prayer seems marked by a beautiful humility. They do not ask for mere justice, they do not ask to be blessed in proportion to their deservings. In simple faith they plead, "Jesus, Master, have mercy on us."

(3) Not only do these men pray, but they also obey. This is, indeed, the supreme proof of their faith. When

they succeed in winning the attention of Jesus, he does not at once touch them into purity. He rather lays upon them a somewhat bewildering command. He tells them to go show themselves to the priests. Now, that is what a leper was to do after he had been cured. But these are told to go while they are still loathsome with their disease. How futile and foolish it seems! Of course nothing can come of it. But in spite of its seeming futility, they obey. They cannot believe that Jesus is merely mocking them by sending them on a fool's errand. They obey because they believe.

4. Finally, they are alike in that they all find healing. How hopeless they seem as they set out upon their journey! But they have not gone far before something happens. The path of obedience is forever the path of healing and the path of discovery. "It came to pass that, as they went, they were cleansed." That was true of the Samaritan, it was also true of his companions. All feel new life pulsating in their veins. Each looks with wide-eyed wonder into the face of the other, seeing what he feels is too good to be true, yet knows is true, both for himself and for his fellows. Thus we see that they are alike in their need, alike in their eagerness for help, alike in their faith, alike in their healing.

II

But here their likeness ends. Here they come to th\

parting of the ways. Having been healed, what do they do?

The conduct of the majority is vastly disappointing. They stand upon the highway just long enough, I imagine, to realize the marvelous change that has come to them. Then with feet made nimble by joy, they continue their journey. "I have not seen my farm for a whole year," says one, as he hurries away. "I have not been to my place of merchandise for even longer," says another, as he follows. "It has been weary months since I felt the hug of my wife's arms and the kiss of my baby's lips," says yet another. Then he, too, is off. By and by all have gone, hot-footed, and the road is empty.

No, that is not quite true. One man is left. He is looking up the road where his companions have just vanished. There is a tender joy in his face, not unmixed with bewilderment. "I, too, have a business that I have not seen for many months," he murmurs to himself. "I, too, yearn to see again those I love. But there is something even more pressing than all this. I must first go back to the Man who has cured me, who has given me back my life, and tell him of my appreciation." So he turns back, even though he has to turn back alone. He makes his way to Jesus, and in an abandon of gratitude falls down at his feet, giving him thanks.

There you have the picture—ten go to beg, only one returns to praise. A small minority, we have to confess, but what a magnificent minority! Was I not right 'in saying that this man is worth knowing? He is only a Samaritan, but he towers above his fellows as Pike's Peak above a molehill. But why is this the case? What is wrong with these nine? Why do they seem such pathetic dwarfs as we look at them? It is not because of any unkind word they said to the One who healed them. It is rather because they simply said nothing at all. They took their priceless gift and went their way in silence. And why do we honor this nameless Samaritan? It is not because he was vastly rich or vastly clever. We honor him because he knew how to say that gracious and heartening word, "Thank you."

III

But why was the one grateful and the nine not?

It was certainly not because of any difference in their circumstances. These were the same. If this one had been cured and the nine left to die, we could have thus explained it. But they were all healed. The truth of the matter is that real gratitude is seldom born of circumstances. If such were the case, we could take the rich, the strong, the successful, and put them in one group, and put the poor, the weak, the failures, in another and say, "These sons of good fortune are thankful, while these unfortunates are not." But we can make no such easy division. When we face the facts we find that many peevish ingrates are whining on the sunny side of the street, while many of their less fortunate fellows are giving thanks among the shadows.

Why then, I repeat, the gratitude of the one and the ingratitude ⌐ the others?

1. To take the most charitable view: Maybe these nine were really grateful at the beginning, but were not so demonstrative as the one, and, therefore, did not give expression to their gratitude. I am mindful of the fact, of course, that one may be grateful without saying so. We hear of such gratitude every day. "He knows I am grateful," we say glibly. "She knows how thankful I am." Had you met these nine, and listened to their story of the amazing mercy that had been shown them, and had asked, "Did you go back and tell the Master how grateful you are?" what would they have said? "No," they would have answered. Then they would have added these familiar words, "But he knows that we appreciate what he has done."

But the trouble with the type of gratitude that we never express is twofold. First, it lifts no load, brings no joy, dries no tears. For though we say of our friends, "they know," as a rule they do not. Even when they do know they are greatly heartened by hearing us say so. This is true even of our Lord. He knows, yet he says, "Let the redeemed of the Lord say so." Second, such gratitude is sure to be a sickly plant that will soon die for lack of sunshine. For you might as well try to grow lovely roses in the darkness of a dungeon as to grow gratitude in a heart that never gives it expression. It is likely, therefore, that the nine smothered their incipient gratitude under a blanket of silence. By refusing to give thanks, they soon brought it about that they had no thanks to give. But this wise Samaritan made his gratitude to grow by giving it expression.

2. Then, the nine may have become so absorbed in the gift that they forgot the Giver. That often happens. I remember a kindly gentleman who was a frequent visitor in our home when I was a small boy. His coming was a great event for me because he almost always brought a gift of candy. But one time he failed. At once my enthusiasm waned. I remember with shame that I let him know that it was not himself in whom I was interested, but in what he brought. So it may have been with these nine. A little while ago they were facing toward the night, now they are facing toward the morning. Possibly they have become so intent upon this new life that is now theirs that they have forgotten all else, even him who made that new life possible.

But this Samaritan—did he not thrill over his gift with joy unspeakable, even as his companions? Indeed he did. Not only so, but I am sure that his joy was far greater than theirs. This was the case because he rejoiced not only in the gift, but even more in the Giver. Instead of allowing the gift to become an obscuring mist to hide the face of Jesus, he made of it a veritable sunrise to give him a clearer vision of that face. He could never think of his blessings without thinking of God, and he could never think of God without giving him thanks. Indeed thanking ever follows thinking as naturally as night follows day.

3. Then it is possible that these nine lost their gratitude in a fashion less worthy still. Instead of becoming so absorbed in the gift that they forgot the Giver, they may have forgotten both gift and Giver in their contemplation of the cost of the terrible tragedy through which they had passed. You see they have suffered in body and mind. Their sickness has doubtless also brought financial reverses. Perhaps from places toward the front, they have fallen to the rear of the procession. They have passed from wealth to want. And though they are now cured, they cannot forget this. They so fix their minds upon their losses that they forget their gains. They are so obsessed by what they do not have that they become unmindful of what is actually theirs. This is a blunder that is all too common. It is also one that is ever a deadly foe to gratitude.

Now, the attitude of this Samaritan was beautifully different. He, too, has suffered. He has passed through dull, gray days and bitter black nights, even as his companions. He has also experienced the same tragic losses. But now that he is cured, the bitterness of his yesterdays is all forgotten, or remembered only to add to the sweetness of today. His heart is so full of glory of the gains that have come into his once empty hands that there is no room for a single pang over his losses. He finds the treasure that is actually his so satisfying that he has never a covetous glance for that which belongs to another. Thus, while the hearts of his companions are empty of gratitude his own is so full that it overflows like a gushing spring.

4. It is even possible that these nine may have taken their healing as a matter of course. True it came about rather suddenly. True, also, it took place quite soon after their interview with Jesus. Still, they may have persuaded themselves that it was their time to recover, and that it would have been all the same if the Master had never come their way. This would have been quite stupid of them, it is true. But let him that is without this same sin cast the first stone at them. For we receive blessings just as signal as theirs every day. "His mercies are new every morning." But because these blessings come to us through natural law or through human hands we often take them for granted. We fail to see on them any slightest finger marks of the good hand of God. Therefore, with this disappointing majority, we miss the fine privilege of giving thanks.

But what the nine took as a matter of course, the one took as a matter of God. This he did, not because he was more blind and superstitious than his fellows, but because he was more clear-eyed and sane. A man is not necessarily a genius because he reads God out of his own universe. To fancy that you have discovered a mirage where others have found a fountain is not an infallible proof of great intellectuality. Some men of great ability have missed God, but their vast ability was not the cause. For every one who has lost God through too clear thinking, millions have lost him through too muddy living. This healed man had received something. So have we. "What have you," I ask in the language of Paul, "that you have not received?" The only answer is, "naked nothing." From whom have all our blessings come? They have come from God. This is true though they have generally been mediated to us through human hands or through natural law. Such was the faith of this wise Samaritan. Therefore, when he saw that he was healed, he turned back to fall on his face at the feet of Jesus in humble thanksgiving.

5. Possibly the supreme reason that these nine were wanting in gratitude was their conceit. It would seem that they were all Jews. Since this was the case they felt themselves far above the Samaritan with whom they had been compelled by their common misfortune to associate. When they were cured they may have taken it as no more than they deserved. They may have gone so far as to give all the credit to themselves, each saying with a prideful swagger, "You can't down me." Millions have been just that silly. Take the Rich Fool, for instance. His fellow-workers had been loyal, sunshine and rain had come in just the right proportions. Therefore, he thought within himself, "How thankful I ought to be!" No, he was far too conceited for that. He only sprained his arm pat-

ting himself on the back, saying, "I, I, I!" Of course he was not grateful. Conceit and gratitude seldom home in the same heart. But this Samaritan was humble-hearted. Therefore he made his boast in the Lord and in him only.

IV

Now, whether we have read aright the causes of the ingratitude of the nine, of this at least we may be sure, that their ingratitude was very real and very ugly. By it they robbed both themselves and others. There is more than a hint of tears in the Master's question, "Were there not ten cleansed? But where are the nine?" By their failure to give thanks they grieved the tender Heart that gave them healing. They taught him "how sharper than a serpent's tooth it is to have a thankless child." They grieved him yet more because their ingratitude made it impossible for him to give them the abundant blessing that he was eager to bestow.

But how beautifully different is this Samaritan! How he heartens us after all these centuries! How heartening he was to Jesus! For, if there is a touch of tears in the Master's voice as he misses the nine, there is surely an abounding joy as he welcomes the one. Then, incidentally, how vastly this grateful man enriches himself! For, by thus returning to give thanks, he adds to the joy of his healing the joy of a growing gratitude. He also adds to the joy of a growing gratitude the joy of an abiding service. Thus also he makes it possible for the Master to give to him a spiritual wholeness to which he must otherwise have remained a stranger. Truly it is good to give thanks unto the Lord. Therefore may we today find our places beside this wise Samaritan and join him in his high service of praise.

XVI

CHRISTMAS WITHOUT CHRIST
(CHRISTMAS SUNDAY)

"There was no room for them in the inn"
LUKE 2: 7

I

HERE IS A STORY WHOSE PATHOS SEEMS TO DEEPEN with the passing of the centuries. The angel of suffering has come to Mary, and her brow is crowned with the sweet radiance of motherhood. In her arms is a little child. That Child is Heaven's King, and the King of this world, and of all worlds. It was of him that the prophet sang: "For unto us a Child is born, unto us a Son is given: and the government shall be upon his shoulder: and his name shall be called Wonderful, Counsellor, The Mighty God, the everlasting Father, the Prince of Peace." He is the Word made flesh that has come to dwell among us, full of grace and truth.

His birth is an event so glorious that all Heaven is athrill with the wonder of it. A star is pointing to the manger cradle with fingers of light. An angel is proclaiming the glad tidings of great joy in words that never lose their sweetness: "For there is born unto you this day in the city of David, a Savior which is Christ the Lord." A wonderful choir from the land where everybody sings is serenading our discordant world with celestial music, praising God, and saying, "Glory to God in the highest, and on earth peace!"

But the wonder of Heaven is little shared by our sin-darkened world. It is true that a few wise men are following the pointing finger of this star, and will soon come to offer their gifts of gold, frankincense, and myrrh. Also a little handful of shepherds who have heard the angel's sermon, and have believed it, are saying one to another: "Let us now go even unto Bethlehem, and see this thing which is come to pass, which the Lord has made known unto us." And they come and find the Child, and finding him, they find a new day. They find Christmas with its passion for giving. Therefore they make known abroad the saying that was told them concerning this child. But the great world passes on its way with unseeing eyes. And this innkeeper who is so close to this great event, who might have had Jesus born within his own home, misses it altogether. In fact he passes through these tremendous hours as utterly unmindful as the dead that anything out of the ordinary is taking place. In his blindness he throws Heaven's supreme gift into an old outhouse, because there was no room at the inn.

Since that distant day, this Child has grown to man-

hood. He has spoken as never man spake. He has
shown himself to be the wisdom of God and the power
of God. He has gone to the cross for man's redemption. He has broken the bonds of death. He has lifted
empires off their hinges and changed the whole course
of human history. Today he comes to us as the Christ
of experience. He accounts for all that is best and
most beautiful in our world. He accounts for that
which was most kingly in your father and most queen-
ly in your mother. Millions have been able to sing of
him out of their own vital experiences:

> "I know not how that Bethlehem's Babe
>   Could in the Godhead be;
>   I only know the Manger Child
>   Has brought God's life to me.
>
> "I know not how that Calvary's Cross
>   A world of sin could free;
>   I only know its matchless love
>   Has brought God's love to me.
>
> "I know not how that Joseph's grave
>   Could solve death's mystery;
>   I only know a living Christ,
>   Our immortality."

But in spite of all this, for vast multitudes this holy
season will be Christmas without Christ, a mere shadow without the substance, a corpse with all life and
beauty gone away. This will be true not simply for
those who have never heard the gladsome story of the

coming of the King. It will be true not alone of those who, having heard, for one reason or another, have failed to accept it. It will be true even of many of us who have heard the good news with joy and have received it and pledged our allegiance to the King. I sometimes fear that we who call ourselves Christians are least Christian during Christmas. There are those who permit themselves debaucheries at this holy season that they do not permit at any other time during the year. There are those who prepare elaborate feasts, and then shut the door in the face of the Guest of Honor. Of course there are many winsome exceptions. Much will be done this Christmas upon which our Lord can smile. A million childish eyes will sparkle, and a million childish hearts will thrill with joy. Of this he will be glad. But still there will be a multitude far too large who will have little or no room for Jesus.

II

Why did not this innkeeper make room for Jesus? Why do not we? There are many possible reasons. I am going to mention only three:

1. This innkeeper may have failed to make room because he was not expecting him. He perhaps had neither thought nor hope of his coming. This is certainly the case with multitudes of us today. We have, in large measure, lost our expectancy. We are exceedingly short on hope. This is one of our predominant characteristics. Very few of us are standing upon

our watchtower, scanning the horizon in the faith that something big is about to take place. Our attitude is just the opposite to that of the Early Church. These first Christians lived on tiptoe of expectancy. There was a word that was constantly upon their lips, that was "Maranatha"—"The Lord is Coming!" They greeted each other with that bracing word when they met in the morning. They cheered each other with it as they went to face death, or horrible tortures worse than death. It was often the password by which they gained admission to secret places of worship. At any moment, they felt, the Lord was likely to come in glory upon them.

This also should be our attitude. One of the supreme needs of the Church today is the recovery of its lost note of expectancy. Our lack of hope may defeat our Lord and shut him out of our lives as effectively as our positive sin. We read of a certain village of the long ago that Jesus visited, but no big and transforming deeds were done there simply because the villagers expected nothing at his hands. We see all too few deeds of might being done by him in our desperate days, and for the same reason. For he is certainly still abroad in his world. Every day he is knocking at the door of our hearts. Every hour he is seeking admission into our perplexed and troubled lives. There is no slightest doubt that he will call on every one of us at this Christmas time. But our lack of expectancy may cause us to shut the door in his face.

Let us, therefore, be looking for him. He will not fail us. For his promise is sure: "They shall not be ashamed that wait for me."

2. Then, this innkeeper may have shut the door in the face of Jesus because he did not recognize him. You see he came to him as the unborn Christ. He did not have your chance and mine. But his failure to recognize Jesus was perhaps due far more to the fact that he was not expecting him than to the guise in which he came. That is almost always the case. It is so easy to fail to recognize one whom we are not expecting to see. After Jesus was crucified, two of his heart-broken friends were on their way back home. There was nothing else to do now that their Lord was dead and all their glad hopes had come to nothing. But as they went their tearful way, Jesus himself drew near and went with them. Not only so, but he entered into conversation with them. But they failed to recognize him. This, because their lack of expectancy had put out their eyes.

But there were those in that distant day who did recognize him, though they saw him disguised as a little child. The sainted Symeon was of this elect group. How did he manage it? Luke lets us into the secret when he tells that Symeon was "on the outlook for the Consolation of Israel." He had read the promises. He had believed them. He had become convinced that he should not die till he had seen the coming King. Therefore, he wakened morning by morning, as children waken on Christmas, full of eager hope. Then one day he went to attend a service at the Temple. To many this was just another service, but not to him. For as he worshiped, he saw a peasant woman enter with a little Baby in her arms. How ordinary they seemed to the crowd! But this expectant saint was able to recognize in that little Child the Anointed of Jehovah. And having recognized him, he at once took him into his arms and into his heart. Then in the realization that the big dream of his life had come true, he burst into a song of sheer gladness that lives to this day: "Lord, now lettest thou thy servant depart in peace, according to thy word: for mine eyes have seen thy salvation."

I do not know in just what guise our Lord will knock at your door and mine at this Christmas season. He may come through a gnawing hunger and a burning thirst. He may come through the consciousness of our weakness, or a sense of the sheer futility of life as we are living it. He may come through some call to service. He may come in the guise of a little child needing our help and saying, "Whoso receiveth one such little child in my name receiveth me." But in some fashion he is sure to come. If we are expecting him, we shall likely recognize him, and recognizing him, receive him.

3. Perhaps this innkeeper did not open the door to Jesus because he did not want him. Certainly that is the case with many of us. By this, I do not mean, of

course, that we would not desire Jesus as our guest if we could have him on our own terms. But we cannot do this. A gentleman drove a sport model automobile up in front of my home sometime ago, and hurried in with the announcement that I was in the X car class, and that because his company was eager to have me drive their car, he would sell that one to me for the meager sum of four thousand dollars. My answer was, "I do not want it." By this I did not mean that his car was not desirable. I did not mean that I would not want it if the price had been four thousand cents, and the company had promised to endow it. But what I did mean was that price and upkeep taken into consideration, I did not want it.

This is too often the case with regard to Jesus. There are guests that some of us insist upon entertaining with whom he flatly refuses to associate. To such he is nothing more than an embarrassment. This has always been the case. When Herod heard of him from the wise men, he did not burst into song—he was merely troubled. When the inhabitants of Gadara learned of the marvelous cure he had wrought on an insane man, also of what had happened to a certain herd of hogs, they hurried to him, not to beg him to abide with them and work other cures, but rather to depart out of their coast. The Jewish nation did not want him, though they had looked forward to his coming for long centuries. About the saddest sentence ever written is this: "He came unto his own, and his own received him not."

What guest will you entertain at this Christmas that will make the presence of Jesus in your heart an impossibility? When Paul preached to Felix, his word was with power. The heart of Felix was deeply stirred. He was made to tremble at the realization of the ghastly mess he had made of his life. He was doubtless made wistful, also, by the recognition of the finer manhood that might be his through Jesus Christ. But he had another guest in his heart, and that guest was lust. He could not give up the woman with whom he was living in adultery, so he said, "Go thy way for this time."

Is that your case? Do not be shocked. I am not accusing you of being guilty of the same sin as Felix. But other more decent and respectable sins may shut Jesus out of your life just as effectively. How charming was the Rich Young Ruler! How eager he was to have eternal life! How courageously he ran down the road, blue blood that he was, to kneel at the feet of a man whose palms were calloused by handling the tools of a carpenter! How clean he was! When Jesus put to him the moral law, he could say that he had kept it from his youth. But when the Master told him how he might have life, saying, "Go, sell that thou hast, give to the poor, and follow me," he went away. He had another guest in his heart. It was the love of gold. It was a decent enough love in the eyes of men, but it shut Jesus out of his life as genuinely as lust shut him out of the life of Felix.

Then, if there are those who do not want Jesus because he is too exacting, there are others who do not desire him because they fail to see that he is infinitely rewarding. He brings treasures with him of priceless worth. His coming means the coming of peace. He makes real to us the song that the angels sang above the starlit heights of Bethlehem. He brings us the spirit of Christmas which is the spirit of giving. He enables us to do for the world, in some measure, what Mary did in the long ago, to give it a living Christ. This he will do for you. This he will do for every expectant soul that refuses to shut the door in his face.

It is said that years ago a French nobleman was spending a few days in Paris. One night as he sat in a certain park of the city he was charmed by the music of the nightingales. He then thought of his own vast estate with its lovely parks, and wondered sadly why no nightingales spilled out their heavenly music there. When he went back home, he discovered the reason. His parks were infested by birds of prey, screaming hawks and hooting owls. He, therefore, set hunters to work killing these evil birds till not one was left. Then, one night he heard the song of a lone nightingale. The next night, there were others. Today his once song-less parks are known as the Garden of the Night-ingales. A kindred transformation Christ waits to

202

work in your heart and mine if we only receive him as our Guest.

III

How may we receive him? All he asks is that we be willing. If we can sing with genuine sincerity, "Come to my heart, Lord Jesus, there is room in my heart for thee," that is enough. In one particular the story of the Garden of the Nightingales breaks down. We do not have to kill or drive out all the birds of prey that are in the garden of our hearts before Jesus will come in. We only have to be willing to let him drive them out. One of the most beautifully suggestive names given our Lord by the holy men of old is the "Dayspring." The word is in itself a poem. It flashes with light. It thrills with the song of awakening birds. It is sweet with the perfume of flowers freshly baptized in dew. "Dayspring" means the dawning. It is the sunrise. And when Zacharias spoke of the little Baby that was soon to be born at Bethlehem, he said, "The Dayspring from on high shall visit us." This amazing Christ is not simply to be a new star in our sky. He is to be a sun, even the Sun of Righteousness, bringing healing in his beams.

Now, since he is the Dayspring, the Light of the world, we do not have to coax him to enter our hearts. We no more have to coax him than we do the sunrise. When a few hours ago the sun looked through the gates of the morning, all we had to do in order to have it flood our homes and make them radiant was to lift the blinds and fling open the doors. And that is all we have to do in order to have the Sun of Righteousness as our guest. We do not have to persuade him. He pursuades us, "Behold, I stand at the door and knock: if any man hear my voice. and open the door, I will come in to him, and will sup with him, and he with me."

For many, doubtless this will be a rather trying and lonely Christmas. There is a grave out in God's acre and a wound in your heart that were not there a year ago. Some will feel the pinch of poverty and will grieve that they have so little to give. Some will be forgotten and will be desperately lonely. But whatever may be your circumstances, there is One who will remember you. However humble your home, there is one Guest that will, if permitted, take up his abode with you. We may all have Christ, and it is his presence that makes Christmas. I once saw a little girl trying to put a bit of soiled note paper into a mail box. It was a letter to Santa Claus, she told me. But tiptoe how she might, she was not able to reach high enough to mail her letter. I went to her assistance, but I am afraid that even then it never arrived. But the smallest of us is able to reach high enough to lay hold on Christ's hand, for he comes down to walk with us and to home in our hearts. Receive him as your Guest, and nothing can prevent you from having a happy Christmas."